Magdalen Smith is Diocesan Di
in the Diocese of Chester. She
arts and is interested in the di.̣..̣.... ....
temporary culture. She is a retreat leader and spiritual director,
and the author of *Steel Angels: The personal qualities of a priest*
(SPCK, 2014).

FRAGILE MYSTICS

Reclaiming a prayerful life

Magdalen Smith

First published in Great Britain in 2015

Society for Promoting Christian Knowledge
36 Causton Street
London SW1P 4ST
www.spck.org.uk

British Library Cataloguing-in-Publication Data
A catalogue record for this book is available from the British Library

ISBN 978–0–281–07384–9
eBook ISBN 978–0–281–07385–6

Typeset by Graphicraft Limited, Hong Kong
First printed in Great Britain by Ashford Colour Press
Subsequently digitally printed in Great Britain

eBook by Graphicraft Limited, Hong Kong

Produced on paper from sustainable forests

For my husband, Paul

Contents

————◆————

Introduction
Reclamation

Reclamation is big business these days. Salvaging items that once were useful, stylish and spoke of a life that had 'arrived somewhere' is now a common pastime in our culture. Words like 'retro' and 'vintage' have become part of our domestic vocabulary. George Clarke, British architect, writer and television presenter, encapsulates this in his series *George Clarke's Amazing Spaces*. Clarke follows people who buy dilapidated 'spaces', be they buses or shepherd's huts, which are then transformed into restored and refreshed working environments, everything from ice-cream vans to fishing lodges. Bunting, Victoriana and 1950s dresses abound and new life grows from what feels tired and hopeless. The results feel invigorating for those watching and are clearly a delight for those who work hard at the transformation of such spaces and places. Perhaps there is an instinct within us all that finds such restoration deeply satisfying. Rather than shunting something off to the scrap yard, that thing is made useful, transformed into a working resource once again. And it is essentially a space that brings and gives new life for others, whether it is food, entertainment, rest or simply a quiet place to experience and dwell in.

In a similar way we carry such spaces within ourselves: spaces and places that are in need of being reclaimed, places that will, with some serious work, provide refreshment and new energy for ourselves but also for others. These spaces are the 'God-spaces' that are easily pushed aside, the door shut, like a forgotten box room. In our age of busyness, these spaces are, like the vintage car that stays locked in the garage for years, in danger of remaining something that we just tinker with occasionally. In an often frenetic culture we need to begin our own spiritual salvage of this inner resource for our own survival and delight. But, like the owners of the spaces in the TV series, it takes recognition to see beyond the present to the potential beautiful resource that is within. For us the hard work is not in sanding, painting and kitting out, it is in the reclaiming of a part of our life that is slowly but most certainly slipping away from our faith and priesthood as other more beguiling activities lure us, seductively, into an apparently more meaningful and worthy existence.

As Christians and priests we are called to pray; praying is a core part of what we do and promise to do. Praying over time should slowly but surely change us, should transform our personhood, our outlook, our ingrained character traits. It should expand who we are to embrace those difficult to love and challenging to negotiate. Prayer should give us the strength to cope with the difficulties of life and to see its profundities in ever new ways. Prayer should be more than reeling off requests or the dogmatic promises of ordination vows. It should be the ongoing unfolding of the living God – both within us and in the recognition of God's activity in those people and projects we involve ourselves with. It should transform our inner spaces so that we have a voracious appetite for life generally as well as hope in a world where others see only despair. As clergy we are called to help others see and understand God, to feel and know his presence in their lives, in head as well as heart. We are called to model such a presence so that others can be enabled and helped to feel it too, however imperfectly.

But there is a problem. In a recent reflection, Angela Tilby bemoaned the supposedly unrealistic adverts for priestly leaders which occupy the back pages of the *Church Times*.[1] 'It seems barely worth applying for advertised posts unless you are gifted, innovative, dynamic, passionate, committed, energetic, collaborative, resilient,' she said. Our parishes sometimes feel so confused, and desperate to solve the problems of church growth, of finance or creativity, that they believe that if they can lure the right miracle-worker then such a person will sweep in and make everything better. According to these descriptions, clergy really do have to be *everything*, all singing, all dancing, messianic jack of all trades, hopefully with a bit of spirituality (whatever that means) thrown in. She makes the point that such adverts develop the feelings of insecurity commonly held among clergy who feel the oppressive weight of such unrealistic desires. Worse still, such requirements tap into the vaguely saviour-type beliefs that some secretly have about themselves.

Subsequent responses to her article asked the question, 'What is wrong with us being aspirational as ecclesial leaders?' There is nothing wrong with being aspirational, inspired and capable, with an ability to 'multitask'. Many would say, 'What is wrong with the Church asking for the best, the ideal, because this is what all of us are called to do on God's behalf?' But such ideals become debatable as we try to pack into our personhood more and more dynamic qualities, resulting in there being less and less time potentially to concentrate on just 'being', the first stage of being with God. The words in the quoted advert have highly 'active' connotations too. Many of us are acutely aware that we are facing a revised horizon in terms of our Church's future and are having to reassess much of what we formally took for granted in all sorts of ways. We are finding it necessary to teach the 'basics' of faith more, to create more sources of income to finance many aspects of ministry, and to spread our leadership far more thinly than we did before. Sometimes we find ourselves falling headlong into an idolatrous abyss, which surrounds us with the belief that it is all ultimately up to our own efforts to do the work of God, underpinned by the harsh fact that in places the Church is grinding slowly to an exhausted and disillusioned halt.

But what has not changed much, except to increase, is the human desire to seek out individuals who convey something of the divine – people who have enough interior space and calm about them for this to be intuitively felt and sought by others. I am not advocating that as clergy we give everything up to become semi-monastic; this is unrealistic and probably not very brave. But in an era when we, as human beings and spiritual leaders, are often far too busy we have to make some serious choices about how we conduct our lives. In his book *Finding Sanctuary*, Christopher Jamison notes the stark reality that for most of us being busy is actually a state we *choose* in some shape or form.[2] It is also something we find difficult to take personal responsibility for. More subtly, busyness can be used by clergy to justify a life that mostly deals with intangibles, helping us to feel that we are proving to ourselves and others that we are achieving things and moving forwards. Even St Benedict, Jamison says, knew that he could be busy with the wrong things – the 'fleeting and temporal things of this world' rather than the painful business of looking into his own soul and those of his monks.

As leaders there is a very real tightrope to walk these days: how do we live and communicate that we are 'normal', unpretentious strugglers who are not 'holier than thou' and yet are people who feel distinctive because of a sustained and healthy inner life, people mysteriously set aside for 'godly things'? It's a tightrope, too, continuing to walk with the Church as it currently is and knowing when to branch out to reclaim a spiritual tradition that has become buried underneath all our worthy ventures. It is notoriously difficult to combine, or marry, these two parts of who a 'priest' is, and we cannot achieve this without the power of the Holy Spirit. Because we are in a state of crisis, which involves exhausting multitasking, it is my belief that a sense of prayerfulness for ourselves as clergy leaders is slowly diminishing, at least as a major part of ministry. In our desperation to build up our body the ancient sense that God is wonder, mystery, darkness and unknowing is being crushed under stones of certainty and entertainment. Meeting ordinands and established clergy who are aware of this and who promote prayer (or a particular kind of prayer) as the *most* important part of what they do feels, at this present time, unusual.

People of prayer from the Christian past, generically here called 'mystics', understood these pressures very well in their time: the pull and tug of active ministry to keep the show on the road alongside the continuous call to spend time in the quiet presence of God. But they committed much time and energy to developing the hidden and contemplative aspects of God (from where the Greek word *mystikos* derives) so that an experience of Christ – in the Bible, through the sacraments, through image and silent solace – could become a genuine resource for all believers and seekers of the divine. The world we live in is one in which many people, of faith and none, search thirstily for God as well.

David Knowles, in his classic book on the English mystics, *The English Mystical Tradition*, says: 'The word "mystic" and its derivatives, like the almost synonymous word "contemplative", has become in recent times both very popular and extremely ambiguous.'[3] The experience of English mystics of the fourteenth century is characterized by a relationship that was often felt to be deeper and more distinctive than any previous communing with God. Often such experiences proved difficult to describe coherently to others. But widening this out semantically as well as historically, a 'mystic' can include any individual compelled to pray a lot, anyone who is overcome regularly by a sense of the overwhelming wonder and love of God, anyone who develops the ability to find God through dispensing with material and psychological clutter. A mystic can be anyone who enters the struggle to walk away from the powerful hindrance of their own desires and ego, yearning for a new inner freedom. And a mystic is anyone prepared to interpret the darkness of life as a normative place of spiritual reality, a place where the unknowability of God is accepted rather than rejected. And, it could be added, mystics are people who simply have a compulsion to connect with the divine but don't quite know how to do so any more. There are many people, of faith and of none, firmly within as well as on the edge of the boundary that is 'church', to whom this refers right now.

The two strands that form a major part of the mystical tradition also need to be reclaimed for us to develop a living, realistic and healthy spirituality, both corporate and individual, which will help us to walk into the next generation of the kingdom in strength and trust. These two strands are the negative (or apophatic) way and the positive (or cataphatic) way of understanding something of the nature of God. The negative emphasizes the total unknowability of God – the fact that when we attempt to describe the divine we diminish God's nature. This is the tradition also of the 'dark night' of the senses and the mind. Writers such as Meister Eckhart or St John of the Cross exemplify this way. The positive (or cataphatic) way emphasizes the indescribable wonder and greatness of God, challenging the world with an inclusive attitude to love, and an often overwhelming sense of God's love and beauty. Thomas Traherne, Julian of Norwich and Bernard of Clairvaux represent this side of mysticism. In his two books exploring the relationship between mysticism and postmodernism, Melvyn Matthews believes that for too long scholars have interpreted 'the mystical' in terms of a personal 'experience', an individual 'wow-factor' type ecstasy.[4] Rather, he says, for the future health and growth of the Church we should retrieve the ancient understanding of what such a mystical understanding of God might mean and what impact it might have in its corporate life. This is not about spooky, spurious personal experiences but rather developing an awareness that the reality of God is bound up with these two strands in our own lives, in the life of the world and in the life of God who is both independent of the world and deeply embedded in it.

The point about reclaiming these two strands is that they connect with where many people are 'at' or 'not at' with God. God's overwhelming love and wonder is widely felt and understood – from the birth of a child to the scented expectancy of a summer dawn. Groping in the emotional and intellectual dark, desperately listening to where God might be, in pain, anger or confusion but encountering a mystery that actually shouts back in silence and cannot be discerned or deciphered, is the reality for many, however. For mysticism to have any impact within a contemporary church context we need to understand, affirm and thread through our 'ministries' the fact that the life and reality of who God is is both *totally unknowable* and *totally embedded and interconnected* in every part of our life. This is the numinous reality of unknowing, as well as the known, sun-drenched love of a man called Jesus Christ. It is also the reality and complexity of the Trinity. Matthews says that it is the Church that provides that place or moment where many people find an opportunity to recognize something of this; we are empty but refuse to fill that emptiness with our own sound or deception. Essentially, the community of God is the place where we find ourselves able to step into the darkness of God, but in confidence and love, knowing that part of the answer is in and through the person of Jesus.

Developing mysticism in the twenty-first century means that we are made freshly aware of God's overwhelming love for us as well. This might render us incapable of actually describing who God is, rather than being constantly obsessed about defining him. We are also called to be newly tentative and careful in terms of how we talk about God because of God's hiddenness, his darkness and unknowingness. Matthews says that in fact we *ought* to have a problem in talking about God more often than not; this is not something that many of those involved in the public ministry of the Church today readily understand or accept as a ministry that we offer to others.

In terms of our own leadership this feels profoundly counter-cultural to what is often asked of us. We have to be good communicators and know what we believe. We need to have vision and provide answers. Bottom lines are required in terms of belief, and rightly so. We live in a rational and scientific age, which stipulates clear description, insisting on things that can be 'proved' even with mysterious entities like 'God'. And yet our postmodern age harbours many whose experience of God feels acutely real and yet remains unaffirmed by church spirituality and language. Looking back into our Christian past, many of the mystical greats encapsulated both of these traditions within their writings and lived experience. Thomas Merton is a good recent example – someone who enjoyed times of explosive and poetic writing about the overwhelming person of God, while at other times experienced periods of dominant and dark obscurity.

To reclaim both these strands within priesthood and to affirm them as an acceptable place to dwell in our understanding of who God might be is surely an honest and exciting position to be in. It is one, moreover, that will prove helpful to many who understand clearly God's integral life within our world but are actually happy to live in the mystery of this. Matthews says this about these two aspects of Christian mysticism:

> Either our speech is blown apart by the immensity of God or we are struck dumb because we cannot speak of that which is God. These two enthusiasts are twin sisters. The health of the Church requires that these twin sisters should be rehabilitated and once again allowed to walk together. There is deep correspondence between those who cannot stop talking about God and those who are forced to stop talking about God because they cannot find any language which is adequate. So in that sense 'the darkness and the light are both alike to thee'. This in essence is a prayerful way to live and work in dynamic freedom and trust.[5]

As has already been intimated, the representative holy people of today – the clergy – often do not have time to pray regularly, let alone find time to develop the depth that became the experience of the Christian mystics of the past, which forms a large part of our ascetical spiritual history. And if this is the case for those paid and set aside for the specific purpose of prayer, how much more difficult is it for lay people who do not have the luxurious excuse to spend time praying in any shape or form, juggling jobs and families as well as a faith life? But our Church is a living and moving body, and one that progresses. Society and people change, yet we believe in a God who remains constant but manifests himself in ways that are appropriate to every age and context. People are still experiencing God prayerfully and mystically; one of the dictionary definitions of 'mystic' is someone who believes in the existence of realities beyond human comprehension. If our God is to be a reality then our job as leaders is to take time to do some of this for ourselves, to relearn a love of prayer and to reinterpret and name that satisfying mystery for others. And we need an understanding that although prayer is an activity that takes us away from others in solitude and silence, it should ultimately be something that takes us towards them too. The concepts reflected on in this book are ones that ideally have the capacity to become *absorbed* into our humanity and personality, like a subtle flavour infusing a meal, giving it character and sustenance. They are to be existentially lived with and in and through.

This book is entitled *Fragile Mystics* because it is my guess that many Christians – both clergy and laity – have a thirst for experiencing the presence of God essentially in mystery, as opposed to certainty, as did many holy people of the past. I believe that simply to sustain that yearning is to be a modern-day mystic, for many of the former saints felt the same frustrations and asked the same questions of their lives that we are doing today. The difference, as previously stated, is often time: time to devote to exploring such matters in depth. The 'mystics' of the title implies that those who seek to be ever holier are people who experience and feel that expansive love and wonder in a way that asks us to walk away from our own egos and into the darkness and beauty of God. We walk with sometimes halting steps, trusting in the love God has for us and for the world. This is surely at the core of why many of us said 'yes' to the call, starting out on our journey towards ordination. For a Christ-like love and the wonder of the unknown is and must be at the root of all prayer as well as all service.

We have at times a continuous and passionate need to hide away somewhere we feel wrapped in a sense of undiminishing, saturating and accepting love which saves us from a sense of desperation and exhaustion. So we are 'fragile' because we feel the weight of what is on our shoulders. We are aware that it can be difficult to communicate competently the power and presence that we call God, and this is something that feels often obscure, hidden and esoteric to those who are searching. We are fragile because when we lead we feel our own sense of imperfection sharply, often the projection by others of a kind of expected expertise of what 'the holy one' should be or know or say. We seek a new and sustainable freedom in terms of our leadership and a holiness that can be 'built in' to our lives.

Integral to any mystical experience is a recognition that the life of God is embedded existentially within the life of the universe. This book introduces concepts that will feel historically familiar as well as, I hope, fresh and contemporary in the light of our own time and context. These concepts are strikingly countercultural too: developing inner stillness in a society that is internally and physically manic, practising the art of dwelling and staying with something in order to experience the depth of God's life, and deliberately taking ourselves out of our comfort zones for the sake of the love of God and others, to name but three. Each chapter reflects on an important aspect of living a prayerful life, with practical and accessible ideas about how to live these out. The result is to reclaim time to be more reflective, prayerful and contemplative, if this is what we are looking for within our leadership and corporate life, the hole we want to fill. It is also about changing the way we live to develop a distinctive approach and pace for our lives, one that is infused by God and that others take notice of.

The fourteenth century was a period in British history that produced several significantly holy people and shares certain characteristics with our own time. The social backdrop was one of great economic recession, where the demands of war had left the country drained of finances. This was the age of the Peasants' Revolt and there were vicious attacks on the Church and religious orders. In other words, there was deep discontent. Perhaps today such displeasure manifests itself in various forms of vitriol aimed at institutions of any kind, which sometimes include the Church. But it is in such times of spiritual darkness that holiness is born through individuals who can sense and manifest the life of God within their own lives, as well as appreciating the dark mystery of everything that cannot be articulated or explained.

Because of this we need leaders who can affirm people's belief that the person of God is often about a sense of un-articulation and unknowing, as well as always about love, incarnated in the person called Jesus. It is also the case that a great many people already experience the living God but need to make sense of this through conversation with those who might just have recognized it already. But such experiences need living through and naming. Clergy leaders, then, are in the unique position of being able to do this – people look towards us. But we fall down when we do not recognize it because we are living too busily, too certainly and insisting on too much light. All the concepts are linked with the vital element of 'taking time', and without recognition of this will potentially flounder. This harnessing of giving proper time and dispensing with other (sometimes more active) aspects of ministry is paramount to reclaiming a church identity and a leadership that is prayerful.

Most of us who call ourselves Christian have, somewhere along the line, been influenced by someone who showed us God: people who have something about them, people who exhibit a certain aura that makes us want to be with them in their humanity and in their spirituality. Although inspiring just as themselves, they enable us to feel the connection to something greater; in the words of Baron von Hugel, 'that the whole world is shot through with divine light', where the person concerned knows that they are related to and united to that transfigured world. Such people are not easily forgotten and may form a major part of our own vocational and faith journey. For me, one was the priest who introduced me to the beautiful darkness of a Taizé service and who had the most extraordinary gift of acceptance of young people. Another was the white Afrikaans priest I stayed with in South Africa, a silent, prophet-like figure who expressed a deep and defining love for the battered people of his township and yet who couldn't wait to get to heaven when 'all would be complete'. As a Director of Ordinands, I have the privilege of listening to and accompanying many who are exploring a sense of God's call in their own lives. I hope this book will create possibilities for all those who read it, a chance to reclaim and develop a sense of the holiness of God but also a sense of themselves as holy and human people, presenting a way of living that builds us into people who are distinctive as followers of Jesus. I hope, too, that within its pages there is a gentle challenge to all our learned ways of behaviour and leadership that have become unhelpful, or even oppressive, over the last few decades. We have the chance to be such people and to learn to live out something of the spirituality of the mystics in our own age and context. Within this is new fire and potential to affirm that which many already know.

1

Still

Creating a still life

———————

There should be, even in the busiest day, a few moments when we can close our eyes and let God possess us. There should be moments at least when we become more conscious of his presence: when we become conscious of it as the only reality, the only thing that will last forever.

(Caryll Houselander, *The Comforting of Christ*)

In hospital I remember thinking that I have gobbled up life too much. I have gone racing from one thing to the next and never enjoyed the moment.

(Andrew Marr, journalist and political commentator, after his stroke in 2013)[1]

On 21 September 2013 Faith Wambua and her two children went to buy flowers at the Westgate shopping mall in Nairobi, Kenya. She was celebrating her second wedding anniversary. While they were in the building a loud bang made Faith assume there had been some kind of explosion. She got down on the ground, telling her children to do the same. Terrifyingly, Al-Shabaab gunmen had entered the building and were randomly firing on shoppers. Faith, her son and her daughter remained motionless – completely still – for over four and a half hours. Miraculously Ty Shawn, Faith's son, fell asleep for most of this ordeal. Faith's account proved extraordinary reading, especially because in this chilling, life-or-death situation she relates how she prayed continuously.[2] Her words are peppered throughout with a natural trust in the presence of a God who responds in situations of intense crisis such as this, giving to those experiencing them a sense of being deeply held and strengthened for their duration. As the gunman shot a nearby woman, Faith prayed silently, singing a song in her head about the resurrection of hope, a concept particularly important to her. Being still in this extreme situation of unpredictable violence saved the lives of three people.

We live in a world of arbitrariness and volatility. Life often feels manic and frantic to many intelligent people who shoulder much pressure. Most of us are ever rarely physically or mentally still, purely because we are so busy, and our lives are now far more complex than they were a generation ago. It is a well-known fact that technology has caused life to speed up, resulting in us cramming more things into our days (and nights). Saving time should, ideally, mean that we have more time to do 'nothing', but the reality is that we want to use such 'saved time' and so we become more and more active. Even if our bodies are still our minds rarely are, and it takes a concerted effort to calm our thoughts. We are driving ourselves into the ground with work, worries and the endless juggling of the tasks our lives demand. For people of faith prayer offers an alternative state of being – a balm and a calm which connects us with something much greater than any power we might find within ourselves. The great mystics and spiritual teachers, both past and present, tell us that to feel something of the mystery and presence of God begins with a sense of this stillness, but it takes concerted effort. No time-saving short cuts will give us an instant sense of the peaceful presence of the Almighty.

Solitude and silence are integral to the idea of 'still'. 'Still' is where we begin to understand the very purpose of our lives as people. The practice of stillness is vital for our survival as human beings, as leaders for our churches and in a society in crisis. In a different way from the story at the beginning of the chapter, stillness will save our lives. 'Still' stops us in our tracks, dilutes our anger, helps us to relish experiences of beauty and interest, refocuses us and enables God to speak through the chatter of our ever-busy brains, simply by his presence. The great mystic Teresa of Avila, a sixteenth-century Carmelite nun, called the mind a clacking mill that goes on grinding. We cannot stop our thoughts, but spending time being still means that those thoughts can be temporarily put aside so that we absorb rather than continually think. We live in a world obsessed more by expanding our physical experience than deepening our inner lives.

This is one main reason why people come to church these days. Time and time again I hear from parishioners and visitors the simple fact that they have stepped through the doors to get some peace. They regard Sunday worship as an opportunity to focus on something other than their own busy lives: a chance to get off the continuously spinning roundabout. Church – an hour and a half on a Sunday morning – is one potential opportunity to do this. Francis Spufford says this in his book *Unapologetic*: 'We live in a noisy place, inside and out, and the noise we hear pours into the noise we make.'[3] Of course, our services are about so much more than giving our world-weary congregations respite, but when being in church is the *only time* people commit to God, then as leaders we need to think carefully as to whether we are helping or hindering people finding such peace. Our services generally have relatively little silence or stillness – they are filled with words, ritual and theological interpretation which provide stimulation and entertainment. Thomas Merton, in *Contemplative Prayer*, says that to underpin our worship with a sense of inner stillness is vital. 'Prayer does not blind us to the world, but it transforms our vision of the world, and makes us see it, all people, and the history of humankind, in the light of God.' He continues:

> Without this contemplative orientation we are building churches not to praise him but to establish more firmly the social structures, values and benefits that we presently enjoy and that without

contemplation and interior prayer the church cannot fulfil her mission to transform and save mankind. Without contemplation, she will be reduced to being the servant of cynical and worldly powers, no matter how hard her faithful may protest that they are fighting for the Kingdom of God.[4]

In other words, a sense of deep stillness should underpin our public worship and this should be tangibly felt, otherwise our well-intentioned mission activities may potentially degenerate into mere philanthropy. All this begins with fostering and sustaining a sense of our own inner stillness as leaders and as people.

'Still' saves us from the heretical belief that we are completely in control of our lives and ministries; and, more insidiously, that we achieve things in our own strength. The Hebrew scholar Walter Brueggemann sums it up well:

It can be a special temptation of modern persons ... to believe that our life springs from us, that we generate our own power and vitality, and that within us can be found the sources of wholeness and well-being. Against the pervasive biblical insistence that human life is in relation to Another, tempting ideologies around us assert that life is grounded in self.[5]

In the tradition of spirituality, prayer – and particularly prayer in stillness – forms an alternative to our perceived autonomy. Being still becomes part of a deepening awareness of what just might be 'other' to me. The famous command in Psalm 46.10, 'Be still, and know that I am God', exemplifies this very well.

Stillness, if practised regularly, changes the way we think, speak, listen and relate to others. The conductor Claudio Abbado, who died in 2014, used to say that there was a particular sound to snow falling: 'It did not come from walking on it. If you stood on a balcony, too, you could hear it. A falling sound, fading away to nothing, *pianissimo*, like a breath. You could hear it only if you listened to what some supposed to be silence.'[6] The point is that to hear snow falling requires concerted stillness as well. Such stillness is strangely powerful. It even changes the way we eat, preventing us from eating too fast. 'Still' is about making a concerted effort to stop, allowing the physical and mental tension that we carry to temporarily slip away. It is about enjoying dwelling in an inactive and silent emptiness where there is no other agenda. Thomas Merton calls this 'recollection': essentially the knowledge that as Christians we have no other reason for existing except to be loved by God, to feel the experience of this unconditional love and to love God and others in return. 'Still' is about releasing a sense of 'the worthy'; in a state of 'still' there should be no intercessory prayer, and we should resist understanding this time as 'creative space' to think stuff out, even though this may happen as a result. 'Still' essentially is just space – space to put ourselves in God's presence because we are beautiful and loved and so is God. Mother Maribel of Wantage says this: 'Silence is not a thing we make; it is something which we enter. It is always there.' She continues, 'All we can make is noise, and that we do thoroughly these days! We desecrate the silence that is God.'[7] This is synonymous with 'still'.

I have practised this concept of 'still' throughout my life as a Christian and subsequently as a priest. Even practised only erratically it makes a difference to how I live my life and conduct ministry. For stillness is about admitting that I need God and that I need him badly, sometimes desperately, and that I thirst for being wrapped in holy silence. Here is a real example. I was hoping to have a quiet night in with my husband (also a priest) at the end of our post-Christmas break, with a delicious meal and recorded TV. My husband's phone rang. Unwisely he answered it and spent 30 minutes absorbing a tirade from an irrational, angry parishioner. Feelings of fury and deep upset were the result for us both. Half an hour later I found myself at another parishioner's house, sitting on her bed as, sobbing, she poured out her heart to me. I silently prayed that God would somehow pick up the pieces of her broken life as they fell, like plaster from a crumbling wall, in my presence with her. The next morning, after a broken night's sleep, I felt the compelling desire to be shrouded in the presence of God to comfort and sustain me for the next 24 hours. I headed for the place in our house which is my own holy space, and managed 15 minutes of stillness before I succumbed to an insistent door-bell and the postman, who came bearing gifts for my daughter's forthcoming birthday. Nearing the end of that same day my spirit longed for time with God again, with no liturgy, no words, no movement, no sound, no demands, only dark stillness.

With this an important question is, 'How do we make the experience of worship also something of a haven and experience of peace?' Advent and Lent are traditionally seasons where we have the perfect excuse to be reflective, and provide people with such opportunities. Open churches provide a space for this as well, although some are finding it increasingly difficult to gather committed volunteers to oversee the space. But there is nothing like an open church to engender community and public feelings of enormous gratitude. People seem to love – really love – a church that is open, even only a little. I've just volunteered to be on our 'church-sitting' rota, not because I have time but because I want to make time to be more still. The idea of visitors arriving in church and experiencing a clergy person just, well, just 'being there' is perhaps fairly unusual these days, unless your church is a cathedral. For the last few years now I have opened our daughter church one day a week during the four weeks of Advent. This is both an opportunity and an actual 'event' we advertise and invite our folk to; it's called 'Still'. This means that I make the commitment to give up three hours of doing other things in order to sit in church. But it also means that I attempt to stop as leader. Or maybe my stopping is just a different kind of work – the 'being' part of priestly identity which then provides the opportunity for others to experience potential hush and serenity. But even here I cannot be 100 per cent 'still', in this place and time, for I become guardian of the building, the person who changes the music (if we have any), the priest as 'open space' who provides a willingness to listen to those who need to talk (in another part of the building), should the stillness draw out issues brewing under the surface of someone's life.

A few years ago while I was doing some Christmas shopping in Chester I wandered into the city-centre Methodist church, partly because it has a café and I was in need of sustenance. In the church was an installation made by a local community artist. It was called 'Windsails' and took the form of a giant white mobile made from paper, string and other materials.[8] The shapes used were triangular, inspired by the shapes the artist had seen in lobster creels on the island of Lindisfarne. This giant mobile created a reflective and calm environment of contemplation. The overall effect was stunning and mysteriously moving. Several people just sat and looked. Advent is not meant to be a manic time; but for the majority of people 'Advent' does not feature on their landscape of 'getting ready for Christmas'. People often ask me, 'Are you ready for Christmas?' It's a bridge and 'way in' to talking with someone you may feel wary of, and I usually respond with something 'normal' like, 'Yes, I've prepared my services, bought and sent all the presents and I'm doing the food shop next week.' But genuinely preparing is about being still enough to comprehend the impact of God arriving on the planet as a vulnerable and impoverished child. That's being 'ready for Christmas', and without 'still' there's no way any of us can really, truly get to that place.

The art installation made such an impact on me that I arranged with the artist to borrow it the following year. We hung it in one of our side chapels, and people responded to the windsails swaying gently in the natural air currents of the building. It provided a soothing place, somewhere to leave on one side the Christmas busyness we all succumb to, and to think, even just a little, about the 'real' meaning of Christmas and perhaps to experience something of the presence of God.

Pertinent readings were provided but mostly folk came just to sit, look and be still. It was so incredibly simple. Again, Francis Spufford: 'Churches are vessels of hush, as well as everything else they are, and when I block out the distractions, the silence is almost shockingly loud. It sings in my ears.' Such events help us to hear this silence.

Last Lent our church oversaw an art project that collated a series of photographs from a local photographic group and some high school students under the ambiguous title 'Dark Matters', related to the story of Christ's journey to the cross. Images on a continuous loop were shown on an overhead screen. Words were displayed alongside the images as well as available to visitors separately as they came into church. Creating opportunities for 'still' becomes a specific ministry that we organize as leadership, which becomes 'church' for others. Christopher Lewis, in *Dreaming Spires: Cathedrals in a New Age*, points out that those who hold responsibility for buildings need to work hard at reclaiming sacred space, controlling their boundaries so that they remain places where something of the numinous can break through, helped by silence and thoughtfully chosen artistic or other stimulus.

In the New Testament there are two stories about boats caught up in violent storms at sea. One relays the incident when Jesus and his disciples were in a boat in a dangerous squall (Mark 4.35–41). Jesus' words to the billowing wind are simply, 'Be still'. The disciples are gently chastised for not having enough faith. In the light of 'still' here, this passage tells us that we will indeed allow our cares and concerns, the weighty pressures we carry, particularly as clergy, to overwhelm us if we do not understand our need of God. We also need the presence of Christ to *enable* us to be still, just as the storm needed Jesus' presence to command it to cease. And what the disciples do not realize is that even in the turbulence Jesus is there with them; they (as we do) need to 'wake this up' within themselves in order to activate (an ironic word, perhaps) this sense of calm.

In other words, we will not discover 'still' without calling upon the person of Christ.

Another incident of a storm at sea occurs in chapter 27 of the Acts of the Apostles. Paul and some fellow Christians, prisoners of the Roman Emperor, are nearing the island of Crete. This particular storm is alarmingly persistent – it goes on for days – and the desperate crew resort to throwing cargo and equipment overboard. Towards the end, as the ship runs aground, Paul insists that the prisoners eat some food. For us, 'still' becomes about feeding ourselves too – sustenance for frenzied physical as well as soul life. It is also about dispensing with habits (sometimes spiritual) that weigh us down and prevent us from simply stopping, just as the crew in Paul's boat took the brave decision to get rid of things that prevented their boat from navigating a safe passage.

Practising stillness should not be a 'self-help' type of answer to a wearying and demanding life. But we are people who tend to give much of ourselves and need to recognize that it is vital to steep ourselves in God continually, and to give others permission to do so too. In fact, we probably do not do enough to emphasize that prayer can indeed *just* be about being still, experiencing the presence of God. Such recharging means filling ourselves once more to the brim, with the love, the radiance and the energy of God. We can carry this stillness with us, throughout the day, able to draw on a sense of God's presence with us, taking it into whatever situation we find ourselves. More vitally, such stillness will enable us to take a sense of composed calm into situations of conflict and anger. This sense of steeped stillness can be seen in the paintings of the Dutch Masters. Servants whose lives must have been far from relaxed nevertheless encapsulate something of a carried stillness, creating profoundly contemplative images. This is similar to our own clergy lives – as people who are busy with a heavy workload who can, these days, devote only a limited amount of our already crowded diary to prayer. In Vermeer's *The Milkmaid*, for example, we understand something of this contained stillness – a stillness which, ironically, possesses a fluidity that is carried through life. Day after day this servant would have done the same task of pouring milk, and yet here is truly a 'still life' where the task is underpinned with slowness and little frenzy. This is not to romanticize past experience, but simply to recognize that Vermeer captures something profound in his portrayal of hard and busy physical work. As we look at these pictures today, in the twenty-first century, we feel the impact of such tranquillity.

As leaders of spiritual communities we have a unique opportunity to help others relearn how to stop and experience a sense of holy stillness at a deep level. But how do we help others to rediscover stillness in ecclesial environments that often model a sense of purposeful busyness? Sister Wendy Beckett, in her *Book of Meditations*, reproduces a still life by the French Impressionist Edouard Manet, *White Lilac*. In the last year of a cruelly shortened life, Manet painted a number of canvases showing vases of fresh flowers. Beckett suggests that he found great consolation in considering their simplicity and 'singleness'. She says this: 'Silence has something of this function; a simplifying, a beautifying. It reminds us that we have only to be still and let the waters of grace refresh us and the sunlight of peace shine upon us.'[9] When we can allow our minds and our souls to be still, then new vision occurs and we are brought in a renewed way into the presence of God, where a more eternal silence connects.

I write this in the month of November, a time in the natural year that can be heavily still. It is quite remarkable to look out at a saturated world of muted colour and to be aware that nothing, not the lightest leaf, the most fragile twig, the thinnest blade of grass, is moving at all. Such stillness potentially stops us in our tracks as the world seems held in something immense, providing the potential to touch the divine as we realize, along with Meister Eckhart, that 'nothing in all creation is so like God as stillness'.[10]

Still in practice

Individual

- Try to practise pure stillness for 10 to 15 minutes each day. Here are two practical techniques.

  Sit with your back straight, feet on the ground with arms and legs uncrossed. Shut your eyes. Breathe in slowly and deeply. It may help to still your mind by imagining you are breathing in the presence of the Holy Spirit. Exhale slowly, imagining that you are breathing out everything you are struggling with in your life at present, whether these are personal or professional difficulties or both. It's a kind of 'breathe in God' followed by breathing out all that brings us a sense of warring tensions within. Do this several times, but pause for a short time after each exhalation. You will find that at the end of ten breaths a sense of peace will have been built, even if only small. It is good to stay with this moment and to try to enjoy just being 'within' it. If you find your mind wandering, don't feel that you have failed, but refocus on the task in hand.

  Or, again sitting with your back straight, feet on the ground with arms and legs uncrossed, shut your eyes. Beginning with your head and working down, try to identify areas where your body is holding tension. Having identified these spots, mentally imagine letting go of the tension. It is surprising how much tension we actually hold in our heads, for example behind our eyes. Concentrate on all parts of your body, systematically imagining your neck, shoulders, arms, torso, legs, until you reach your feet. Recognize the places of tension and mentally release this. With practice, again you will discover that a sense of stillness develops within and around you through this exercise.

- Some people use words to find a still space within. These two phrases are ones I have found helpful: 'Maranatha, come,

Lord Jesus' (from ancient Aramaic meaning 'Come, Lord') and 'Spirit of the Living God, fall afresh on me' (Taizé).

- It helps if you can find a time to be still at home or in church when you know you will not be interrupted and that no one is likely to invade the silence. Find a place that is not associated with 'work'. Strangely, I don't always find it easy to do 'still' in church because this is a place where I work; often there is the interior anxiety of leading worship, with the responsibility of everything running smoothly. I do 'still' usually in a place at home with the minimum of associations with other things and no technology either.

- If you are a visual person it may help to imagine or remember a place where you have felt very at peace in the past. Imagine being in this place and use alongside any of the above exercises.

Corporate

It can feel slightly daunting for leaders to develop the concept of 'still' among or for large groups of people, perhaps because generally we are becoming less used to it.

- As a leader of worship it is possible to find small 'spaces' within a service to be still and to use silence. I once led a course on prayer in the sermon slot on Sunday mornings for six weeks, practising the techniques collectively for the intercessions. It was quite a daring thing to do, perhaps, but everyone gave it a go, and a good number of people told me afterwards how spiritually strengthened they felt through participating in it. Even for churches where this idea would be impossible, it is nevertheless realistic to pause more, developing periods of silence during the intercessions or occasionally experimenting with larger groups of people using the stilling exercises above. Home and prayer groups are ideal places to introduce stillness, if these are usually 'filled with words' and ideas for activity. The key is to believe in the power of 'still' and pastorally to be there to pick up the pieces afterwards should issues be brought up from within the depths of people's lives.

- Special 'still' services also provide good opportunity for people to learn stillness. Taizé liturgy, with its repetitive chants and use of icons, is a well-established way of doing this, but it can feel alien in certain church traditions.

- Leaders who are governors of schools (in particular church schools) have a positive opportunity to teach the practice of stilling and meditation to children in careful ways. You might like to try some of the above exercises in Sunday Club or your equivalent.

- Try opening your church more often. Explain to volunteers why this is increasingly important to all people whether of faith or not. If this seems completely impractical, then perhaps open at certain reflective times during the church year – perhaps for one morning a week or as part of a focused project that will draw others in anyway. Using visual images in a meditative way will have an impact too, encouraging people to stop and take time to look and dwell in our holy places.

2

Gaze

The lost art of adoration

We talk of God very casually and write about him as if he were a prescription for our ills. Even in church there's less sense of the majesty, the power and the glory of God. The awe has gone out of our worship and the proper fear has all but disappeared from our heart.   (James Jones, former Bishop of Liverpool)[1]

He stepped down, avoiding any long look at her as one avoids long looks at the sun, but seeing her as one sees the sun, without looking.   (Leo Tolstoy, *Anna Karenina*)

In *Gatsby*, Baz Luhrmann's spectacular interpretation of Scott Fitzgerald's classic novel, there is a moment of utter and intense adoration. Gatsby, reunited with his former love, Daisy Buchanan, during an over-the-top afternoon tea, cannot stop gazing at her. He is entranced, not only by her beauty but by the opportunity to reignite his love. She too, slightly bewildered by the circumstances, finds herself captivated in his presence. The scene is mesmerizing. If there could be a personification of human adoration it would be how Gatsby (played by Leonardo DiCaprio) looks at Daisy, with a focus that does not waver. He is, at that moment, utterly absorbed, taken to another place of future possibility. Many of us have experienced something like this – a time in our life when we were dizzily in love with someone or something, a head-over-heels state of mind and heart that leaves us unable to concentrate on much else.

The concept of adoration is an ancient one in our spiritual tradition. When I was confirmed in the 1970s the fourfold pattern of 'ACTS' as an approach to prayer was still prevalent in the classes. We learnt about Adoration, Confession, Thanksgiving and Supplication (or asking for things). Contemporary worship experience feels like the first of these is rather missed out; the other three are embedded firmly in our collective prayer life and worship, but there is a sense that Adoration, even though its presence is asserted in our common liturgy at various points, is less dwelt upon and less understood as a contemporary approach to God. Adoration should be the primary reason, conscious or not, that we come to church – the idea that worship is about giving God the worth that he deserves, expressing our heartfelt love, gratitude, devotion towards him, just because God is God. Yet the idea of looking at God just for God's sake alone feels slightly strange, maybe even alien to many a contemporary spiritual mindset. Interestingly, since the beginning of the nineteenth century the common usage of the word 'adore' has apparently decreased by 50 per cent, and it is my belief that an understanding of adoration is slowly and surreptitiously slipping from our personal and corporate worship and prayer life as Anglicans. Eventually this affects our theology and how we understand God manifests himself in our life and world. It's either this or the fact that the concept of adoration has been subsumed, subtly changed into other ways of us experiencing the presence of God. Perhaps we are a little bit embarrassed about saying that we 'adore God'.

Adoring anything is primarily a relationship of love – that utter, loyal, all-consuming, walk-to-the-ends-of-the-earth-type love, whether it's for a moment or for an eternity. Most of us need and desire this love as part of our human experience; we identify with that compelling feeling that comes from deep within us. The idea of adoring is clearly understood because it is how we may feel about others and links with the idea of loving purely, without judgement. St John of the

Cross says that if we can love in such a focused way through adoration, then our humanity and spirituality automatically expand. 'The more this kind of love grows the more our love of God grows with it; and the deeper our love for him the more we shall love our neighbour for the principle of the same is both.' If we fail to look at others in genuine love then we will fail to love God genuinely too. To adore means loving something just for the sheer fact that it is worth loving because it is amazing, beautiful, compelling, and brings us a joy beyond measure.[2]

Much of the mystical tradition of the past manifested itself through an adoration of the divine in some shape or form. For our faith now it's about us taking time to look at, stay with and focus on God, perhaps through a visual or imagined presence of Jesus, through image or prayer, which opens up an ability to love others and transforms us through the experience. Bernard of Clairvaux believed that the human soul could only get to this point by experiencing the living God, with our hearts as well as our minds expanding how and what we see as we experience life. Thomas à Kempis describes, in *The Imitation of Christ*, the burning love and great affection all Christians have as they receive the sacrament: 'All generations and kinds magnify thy holy and sweet name in great joy and burning devotion.'[3] Teresa of Avila talks about the unexpected presence of God when picturing Christ or when reading about him, 'of such a kind that I could not possibly doubt that he was within me or that I was wholly engulfed in him'. She describes a tenderness in devotion, a feeling that does not come primarily from our own efforts but from the power of God himself. She says:

> We can also do much by rejoicing in the contemplation of his works, his greatness, his love for us, and a great deal more. If to this there be added a little love, the soul is comforted, the heart melts and tears begin to flow. For here (the soul) finds encouragement, and here it finds joy.[4]

A present-day experience was a little like this. One day, before taking a midweek service in a side chapel of our church, I sat and tried to pray. I felt angry and bitter about a particular issue. The last thing I felt like doing was leading people in calm and composed worship, when inside my emotions churned. I sat in silence looking at the central pane in the window – an image of Christ on the cross. Beneath Christ's feet, one of the faithful women friends wraps her arms around Jesus' legs while her other hand covers her face in anguish. I stared at the image with no mental intentions. I stared, not particularly concentrating on my inner attitude. As I gazed I was aware of something changing within me; my inner turmoil and angry emotions began to slip away, absorbed into an expansive framework of love, focused on the figure of Christ on the cross. For me the experience was mysterious but also mystical particularly because of my complete lack of conscious effort. I got up and took the service.

Was this 'adoration'? It certainly wasn't in the sense that I was gazing adoringly at the person of Jesus in the 'right' attitude or with the sugary sweetness of expected reverence my childhood faith might have asked of me. But it just might have been in the sense that I had looked for long enough at a religious image for that image to transform my soul for that particular moment, when it was necessary to lead worship in the right spirit. I am aware that I often do not look properly at some of the people I encounter, or perhaps do not have time to look deeply into a situation to discover where God might be. At the supermarket checkout the other day, for example, I realized that I had packed six bags of shopping, even exchanged pleasantries with the assistant on the till, without actually looking at her face. Something about this fact disturbs me even though I knew I had behaved courteously and pleasantly. Perhaps it is actually because our faith encourages us to look for the person of Christ within each other. Really looking at someone is, of course, an intimate thing to do; by doing so we allow ourselves to be affected, changed by that person's individuality and the issues and emotions they are carrying. I recognize a slight shyness in myself which is afraid of the risk of venturing into the experience of another person's inner dynamics, which is the risk when you really look at and interact with someone else. In 2010 the performance artist Marina Abramovic sat in a gallery in the Museum of Modern Art in New York and invited people to sit opposite her. For approximately three months, for seven and a half hours each day, she gazed into the eyes of whoever had chosen to sit opposite her. Many people recorded the power that this experience had on them and how they realized that to really look into the face of another is strangely challenging as well as potentially moving.

Looking – and dwelling on the looking – stimulates us to ruminate, to chew over things in depth. Repeating the same prayers, looking at certain images, sitting in silence in church, 'somehow helps keep the door ajar through which he may come'.[5] But this involves time as well as focus – two elements that do not always sit easily in our instantaneous and easily bored culture, where we have all the beguiling distractions of social media to hinder the development of our concentration upon any one thing. In the Bible we read of individuals bound up in the pursuit of God as they yearn to visualize the very essence of the divine, which for many subsequently proves too much. Moses veils his own face in order to protect himself from the effects of such a potentially intense experience. Yet 2 Corinthians 4.18 tells us that if we look for long enough on the face of the Lord we will, almost in spite of ourselves, become transformed.

The quotation at the beginning of the chapter speaks of the potential power of looking for long enough at another person to see what this might generate within us – the spark of love, the prick of conscience or the ache of a long-forgotten wound. Within the traditional understanding of adoration is the idea that if we dwell long enough on really getting to grips with who we believe God to be then we give our souls a chance to experience the beauty, the awesomeness, the sacrifice, the general 'everythingness' of God. If that's adoration – and I think it is – then it is robust enough to cope with our 'gaze' when that gaze is one of anger or suspicion or disgruntlement. This kind of sustained looking is necessary for us all if we are serious about Christian faith. We have to be brave enough to look not just at the gorgeous things but at the challenging things as well. Timothy Radcliffe, in his book *Sing a New Song*, says that our eyes need education in order to see God's beauty when it is concealed in the apparently ugly. Our looking requires healing, he says, as well as compassion, which trains our eyes to see the loveliness of God in unexpected places. He speaks of a rabbinic tradition that describes the return of the Messiah, coming back to sit at the city gates in the form of a beggar, expecting that most people will see an ugly man: 'He had no form or comeliness that we should look at him, and no beauty that we should desire him' (Isaiah 53.2). Adoration as a 'subversive' act is an idea developed by Gordon Mursell, reflecting on the adoration of the magi, an act that outrages Herod because it undermines his own despotism. But adoration, he says, also lifts us out of self in order to offer unconditional love and reverence to someone else, to shift the focus away from ourselves: 'Adoration releases the imagination that frees us to dream of a different world. What is, in utilitarian terms, entirely useless is precisely the key and mainspring for personal and corporate change.'[6]

An art gallery is perhaps one place where people do dwell and gaze, where there is the potential to really look at something to the extent that the gazing has the capacity to challenge and change us. I remember discovering the paintings of Mark Rothko – gigantic canvases of concentrated and intense colour. Many people describe looking at Rothko's art as a genuine spiritual experience, enabling them to be absorbed potentially into another reality that feels numinous and sacred. On the walls of the Rothko Chapel, a non-denominational chapel in Houston, Texas, are 14 paintings in varying shades of black. The patrons of the chapel, John and Dominique de Menil, believe that it is only abstract art that can bring people to the threshold of the divine. This introduces the idea that we can experience something spiritual, something otherworldly, by transcending the actual physicality of a piece of art or image. Evelyn Underhill says:

> As we can never know the secret of great art or music until we have learned to look and listen with a self-oblivious reverence, acknowledging a beauty that is beyond our grasp – so the claim and loveliness remain unrealized till we have learned to look, listen, to adore. Then only do we go beyond ourselves and our small vision, pour ourselves out to that which we know not, and so escape from our own pettiness and limitations into the universal life.[7]

This is the fundamental idea behind the figurative iconography of the Orthodox tradition – a discipline that far from being abstract encourages believers to dwell 'in the looking', to adore and revere images of Christ himself. An Orthodox believer said to me recently that looking at an icon was akin to Lucy's discovery of the wardrobe in C. S. Lewis' *The Lion, the Witch and the Wardrobe* – it takes us into another world.[8] And it is a world, moreover, that is just as 'real' as the one we have temporarily left. An icon, then, becomes a kind of 'holy door-way'. In Orthodox spirituality there is the belief that through iconography the ideal beauty of paradise is, in a small way, restored, illuminated to humanity, and made possible by the fact of the Incarnation of Jesus. There shines a divine light through the depiction of a holy image that transfigures and changes the viewer from within. Thus icons become a sacramental presence, a piece of 'heaven on earth', and part of the restored beauty of paradise. They create for those who look on them a tangible stillness, peace and beauty in the contemplation of such images; Orthodox Christians believe that this gradually changes those who contemplate the images, so they become filled with love and reverence for all creation. In this sense it becomes less about the mind's discipline and more about the heart's response to what is God's primary language, with 'everything else being a poor translation'.

This was something of the philosophy behind the music of John Tavener, himself a practising Orthodox Christian, who died in 2013. In a documentary charting his *oeuvre* it was said that his music opened a door to the divine, often with a stillness that seems paradoxical to the whole concept of making music. *Shunya*, for example, is a piece that produces a stillness that appears to go nowhere; rather it hovers in one place in its musicality. Tavener believed that his music did not come from his own genius but was literally dictated to him by divine revelation. Listeners often experience his music as haunting and consoling, sometimes deeply cathartic. His contemporary John Rutter speaks of it as 'somehow belonging to another world'. The singer Patricia Rozario, a leading interpreter of Tavener's works, comments that there are many layers you need to pass through in order to sing the music as he intended it to be sung. So here is the idea of dwelling, experiencing the holy through the exquisite beauty of music in a particular form.

But specifically for Orthodox Christianity, contemplating the image of Jesus enables a person to move beyond the physical icon or image, and to begin to experience the *actual* person and presence of Jesus. This use of art introduces the idea that eventually, if we look long enough, God draws us towards him, not through our own efforts but through the mystery of his power. This, I realize now, was what was happening to me on that morning in church, as I sat steeped in my anger, gazing at the stained-glass crucifixion. Julian of Norwich suggests that prayer depends on facts not moods. Misguided personal effort can degenerate into a kind of spiritual Pelagianism – the idea that all depends on us and that if we fail to keep up our intense concentration for a moment then our prayer must be ineffective. In fact, any prayer we offer does not fail but becomes the link between earth and heaven – prayers, she suggests, that are taken by Christ who understands and uses them as precious and incorruptible treasure.[9]

How can we, as leaders, help to recapture and reintroduce the idea of adoration as a spiritual practice in a way that feels understandable for contemporary Christians, something that helps people to delight in the presence of God within their lives? These days our theological approaches in the Church of England are often 'activist'; much church life suggests that we have to *do* things in order to communicate the kingdom and a God of love. Of course, we do have to do things, but I recognize that this is a dangerous myth within myself, one that easily degenerates into a lack of trust that God is able to work in a transformative way through the experience of dwelling, being, gazing and staying, as opposed to worthy social action. Yet here might lie a potential answer to recapturing the idea of 'gaze'. Providing opportunities that encourage and enable people to look at others and life in general from a changed perspective, in a similar way to how we believe God looks at the world – thoughtfully, with awe, wonder and reverence – is a revolutionary and countercultural approach. My family went on what we described as a 'holiday of a lifetime' last year. The two weeks were jam-packed with the stimulating and problematic richness of human life embodied in the places we visited and people we met. On our return I felt I needed a period to unpack what had been an immense experience, to understand it through different-coloured lenses, to dwell with everything we had done as memories that punctuated the present. Yet for some of our fellow travellers it was clear that although they had greatly appreciated the experience it was, essentially, 'just another holiday'.

Reviving the idea of adoration, of gazing, is vital to the spiritual health of our leadership, our Church and the discipleship of others; it marks us as people who might just have fresh words of wisdom to offer from the 'God-perspective'. Dionysius the Areopagite talks about the presence of God reaching from the lowest to the highest forms of being and yet also remaining beyond everything: 'It gives light to everything capable of receiving it, creating them, keeping them alive, preserving and perfecting them. Everything looks to it for measure, eternity, number, order.'[10] In other words, people are potentially transformed while looking through eyes that are tuned into the holy in its widest sense. In a similar vein, the French philosopher and priest Pierre Teilhard de Chardin describes gazing at a picture of Christ on a church wall. This experience created an atmosphere where 'the entire universe was vibrant'; all emanated from the figure of Christ, whose 'transfigured face drew and held captive my entire attention'. Teilhard de Chardin describes with mystical beauty the experience of gazing at the face of Christ which encapsulated 'innumerable gradations of majesty, of sweetness, of irresistible appeal, following one another or becoming transformed and melting into one another, [they] together made up a harmony which brought me complete satiety'. The writer leaves his picture and very personal vision unsure of whether he had experienced indescribable agony or triumphant joy.[11]

This matters not, for what is clear for this twentieth-century mystic is that he was changed by staying long enough to encounter the holy, absorbing something of God in a way that changed him profoundly. In another meditation, on the monstrance, gazing at the host stimulated an intense feeling of love, 'as was taking place in the domain of love, dilating, purifying and gathering together every power-to-love which the universe contains'.[12] In an interesting recent news item it was discussed that we are so obsessed with taking photographs with high-quality devices, of recording an event, that we ironically miss the experience of the 'now'. Anthony de Mello tells a story of a father taking his children round a museum. He was hurrying them along saying, 'If you stop to look at each thing, you won't see anything!'[13]

The prayer of the mystics of the past progressed from the recited, formal prayers of daily offices towards a more spontaneous extempore approach and finally to wordless adoration, often including a deep sense of love for God and the harmony that accompanied this. Richard Rolle, the fourteenth-century mystic and writer, says in *The Fire of Love*:

> In my prayer I was reaching out to heaven with heartfelt longing when I became aware, in a way I cannot explain, of a symphony of song, and in myself I sensed a corresponding harmony at once wholly delectable and heavenly, which persisted in my mind.[14]

For Margery Kempe, the experience of a God who is a living presence exceeds description, often moving beyond words. Interestingly, in our highly visual culture where many people no longer read books such an approach might have prophetic relevance for us today. Praying unceasingly did not mean an endless stream of words; rather it comprised making a regular effort to spend time 'staying' with God, which gradually develops the habit of desiring this loving presence just for its own sake.

The concept of 'gaze' is about trying to recapture the practice of staying and looking that the mystics and holy people entered into in such depth and detail in the past, partly because they had the time to do so. Gaze today is less the premeditated adoration of previous generations and more a willingness to place ourselves where we are open to feel the nearness of God, be it church or countryside, looking at a specific image or chewing over a particular experience. Gaze is, too, essentially a way of looking. It is the attempt to look beyond beauty or ugliness to see something greater and more profound, through the prosaic as well as the extraordinary. As God's eyes, contemporary Christians can still find ways to look at the world as God does, to push through the cynicism, dismissal and rush with a fragile and tentative vision that asks the world to see it in another way.

Gaze in practice

Individual

- Begin collecting favourite images that are evocative – cards people have sent you and images you can buy (postcards, for example). Use these to look at as prayer. It can be stimulating as well as illuminating to see how, if we look at it for long enough, an apparently ordinary image can become multi-layered and speak to us. Collections of photographs are also good for this.

- Visit your local art gallery, if you have one. Familiarize yourself with what is on display and return to one or two favourite items to look at that might speak to you of God. There is much excellent contemporary and past Christian art around but exhibitions of any type can be potentially transformative. The works of so-called 'secular' artists can be highly spiritual. You might try Chris Gollon, Bill Viola, Mark Rothko, Stanley Spencer, Rob Floyd. A particularly powerful image is Rembrandt's *Return of the Prodigal Son*; or explore more contemporary images by Ghislaine Howard.

- Familiarize yourself with the theology of iconography and spend time looking at an icon when you pray. It's very easy to buy reproductions of these.

- Find a building with stained-glass windows; learn about the images portrayed, and spend time just looking at them.

- Think of somewhere you enjoy being that would provide a quiet, still and contemplative place for you to stay undisturbed for 30 minutes to experience God's presence. You could make a commitment to doing this on a regular basis.

- Take time to look at people more than you normally do, without being distracted by other people. Do this sensitively, and pray that you will experience something of God's presence through looking at and being with them.

Corporate

- Put trust, time and silence into leading the congregation or group to look at appropriate images. People often relish a chance to just sit and 'be', and enjoy looking at images. It can be astonishing how God speaks to people in a variety of ways just through one image.
- Hold a service using Taizé liturgy, or explore holding a service that provides opportunities for people to look at art or listen to music in a meditative way.
- Collect images of Christ. *The Christ We Share*, published by USPG (now known as Us) and CMS, is a wonderful collection of images of Jesus from around the world. These can be used in a variety of contexts.
- Lead a series of meditations or sermons on the stained-glass windows in your church, if you have them.
- Take a group to an art gallery. Do some research beforehand and try to find ways of linking what is on show with faith and our experience of this.

3

Flux
Holy hanging loose

———◆·◆·◆———

I alternate between thinking of the planet as home – dear and familiar stone hearth and garden – and as a hard land of exile in which we are all sojourners.
(Annie Dillard, *Teaching a Stone to Talk*)[1]

The nature of life is not permanence but flux.
(Lord Grantham, *Downton Abbey*, series 5, episode 1)

Grayson Perry – artist extraordinaire and transvestite potter – explored the British class system in a television series on Channel 4 in 2013 called *All in the Best Possible Taste*. In its three episodes Perry visited situations and locations that he identified with the three archetypal class groups: Sunderland (working class), Tunbridge Wells (middle class) and the Cotswolds (upper class). As presenter, Perry, raised a working-class lad, appeared courteous and non-judgemental to the core, entering into each context with relish, mirroring his own prismatic approach to life. As an artist he translated the people he encountered and places he visited into six intricate, high-quality tapestries, with the title *The Vanity of Small Differences*. Two tapestries (each measuring 2 metres by 4 metres) mark a 'phase' in the life of Perry's anti-hero, Tim Rakewell, a working-class boy who through grit, driving ambition and ultimate stupidity marches through his own life with disastrous results. The detail is brilliantly observed, and through it the artist establishes the various environments where people feel they belong and the security that stems from this – from the style of dress for the girls on a night out in the pubs of Sunderland to the vintage 'chic' of the new middle class. Tim's story is heavily based on Hogarth's *The Rake's Progress*, which parallels the consequences of a life lived with exaggerated narcissistic and heady social climbing.

Perry won the Turner prize in 2003. His pottery and tapestry are analogies to the multi-layered nature of life generally. He is convinced that the class system still survives, perhaps manifesting itself more subtly than in previous decades. He concludes that over the past 20 years it is the middle classes that have expanded the most but whose generic identity and interpretation prove to be the most subtle and amorphous. The title *The Vanity of Small Differences* originates from a phrase from Freud in *Civilization and its Discontents*. It alludes to the fact that we most passionately defend our individuality by differentiating ourselves from those we are alarmingly similar to.

As I looked at these works in Manchester Art Gallery a small part of me resonated with the character of Tim. I sense an uncomfortable urge deep within my own psyche to 'get on', to climb the ladder, to have the right 'stuff', to be successful, whatever this means. While there are global ideologies that do not beat the materialistic drum, most of us find such desires hard to push against as we in the West are immersed in a materialistic and ambition-hungry environment. Even as Christian people we find this hard to resist, despite being aware of the biblical background that tells us that making stuff, or 'lifestyle', our god can bring deep dissatisfaction and unhappiness.

The need to own, to possess, to control, to collect, to be acquisitive, to feel we are secure and that we have 'arrived' at a state of stability – all this is a natural part of our (fallen) humanity. We have to work hard at climbing down the ladder, at swimming against a cultural tide that tells us that we are incomplete without the right possessions or jobs or way of living. As people of faith we have to find the energy to 'hang loose' to the things we believe we 'own', letting go of control, be this about material things, roles or people. Many people these days feel an insidious lack of 'security', be it in employment, relationships or future financial security; these form an underlying anxiety that fills up the tiny holes in what we want to be the trusting faith that underpins all our life. Yet underneath all this is a growing countercultural movement that thirsts to live with another consciousness and value system – one to which new monasticism in particular has something to contribute, as well as many contemporary Christian writers and movements. It is interesting that at the time of writing, Justin Welby invited members of both well-established and newer religious communities to Lambeth Palace to share a vision for the future of a way of living, believing that they all have something very specific to contribute that seeks not to possess or control. The scheme is also inviting specifically younger people aged between 18 and 30 to live in community for a year, sharing practical life and prayer.

In actuality, our lives constantly shift and change. Many Christians, leaders or otherwise, believe that living prayerfully at this time in our history requires us not only to live less materialistically but to relearn how to view our lives as fluid and changeful in order to rediscover the presence of God. The fourteenth-century mystic Meister Eckhart talked about God's goodness as being only 'lent' to us; it is not to be our possession but should be developed into an understanding that all of life is essentially gift. Such an approach allows God's activity to feel like holy movement, enabling us to be guided into the ever new, helping us to enjoy the places and communities we find ourselves in, where the underlying dynamic is one of movement and progression, like the flow of a stream. This way of existing is a conscious attitude towards life, an attitude that lives in the now, a dynamic that is open and flexible and is happy to borrow and inhabit space and people freely without ever seeking to possess. I'd like to call it 'flux'.

In an essay entitled 'Renewing the Face of the Earth', Rowan Williams quotes from Leviticus 25 in reminding us that human beings will always be temporary tenants on an earth that ultimately belongs to God. We can never *possess* the land in which we live and thus it is never ours to do just what we like with. He cites the American biblical scholar Ellen Davis, who says that there is a sustained argument in this passage that states that both people and land alike belong to God and in this way neither should possess, 'own' or abuse the other. Williams continues that a right attitude to possession reflects the relationship that God has with all his children, and for humanity to behave differently is to distort what is essentially divine gift:

> To understand that we and our environment are alike in the hands of God, so that neither can be possessed absolutely, is to see the mysteriousness of the interior life of another person and God within it . . . If God's people are called to reflect what God is like, to make God's holiness visible, then just or good action is action which reflects God's purpose of liberating persons and environment from possession and the exploitation that comes from it.[2]

To be a prayerful Christian and to live by example as a Christian leader requires us continuously to attempt to loose ourselves from the bondage of a cultural mindset of possessiveness. The great mystics of the past believed that getting close to God means allowing the power of love to move freely through our souls and bodies. Richard Rohr speaks about God refusing to be boxed in and possessed, God as a verb rather than a noun, 'more a process than a conclusion, more an experience than a dogma, more a personal relationship than an idea'.[3] The Holy Spirit moves through us so that we ourselves are always only the conduits and receptacles; this brings incredible freedom to our weary psyches, which carry the weight of the personal worlds we construct around ourselves. A wonderful simile for the presence and action of God as 'flux' might be the northern lights, which remain a constant phenomenon in our skies and yet when contemplated shimmer and dance in countless combinations of light and colour.

At the heart of such a journey is the need to dispense with the illusion that we are at the centre of our universe and can build a life around this by our own capability alone. Thomas Merton speaks about this pull and tug, ebb and flow of yearning to assert our egos, describing it as a continuous war within us. In *The New Man*, he takes matters back to the Garden of Eden, and the yearning of Adam to possess knowledge that was not his to possess, a kind of blindness that did not understand that the gifts were bestowed upon him by God and could not ultimately be possessed. To try to do so is to misunderstand the true nature of who God is and how he gives to us. What happens, Merton says, is that we rationalize and excuse the lusts and ambitions that arise from our ego as we invent ever new ways of believing that to be happy is to own, to control and to feel 'in charge' – 'the psyche of man struggles in a thousand ways to silence the secret voice of anxiety', he says. When we stop to look inward into how our human experience actually *feels* as we live our lives, we become aware of a distraction, or being forever pulled apart by a multiplicity of worries and pressures that mostly stem from the need to possess and control: 'For our soul and body, created to be a temple of God, cannot help but seem a haunted place after the desecration that has evicted its only rightful dweller. No amount of business prosperity or luxury can hide the abomination of desolation within us.'[4] Bleak, perhaps; but the contemporary film *Noah* (2014) echoes this idea, with its flashbacks of plucking the apple and the hiss of the snake in Eden, suggesting that the ark itself has become the protector of the sacredness of all creation.

But there is another way to live. Merton describes this as a conscious withdrawal from our desire to possess both things and people, turning inwards as we attempt to find again God's presence within the ultimate silence of our deepest selves. We must 'repossess' our own souls, he says, to free ourselves from the anxiety, fear and inordinate desire that our culture presses upon us constantly. And when we have achieved this we are able to live our lives, stepping out of our selfish selves to love others and enjoy life and the spaces and places we find ourselves in freely, enjoying these as 'gift'. This does not come in one revelatory moment of conversion but is the ongoing process of liberation from an attitude that says that everything is 'mine'.

Here a kind of holy inhabiting begins that offers an alternative to personal possessiveness and acquisitiveness. Clergy, along with others, can model this. We might be 'home owners' but we often live 'freely' in a tithed property which, if stipendiary, is not ours. We may remain in one church or position for significant periods of time, but at the back of even the longest-serving clergy person's mind is the knowledge that we are always only 'passing through'. We do not know where the wind will blow us next and we put ourselves and those we love most dearly at the discretion of the Holy Spirit. We are placed to exercise leadership in a particular context and for a specific time, in communities that are made up of solid church buildings but also communities of people who move and change organically because of all kinds of socio-economic factors. Meg Wheatley talks about this in terms of clergy living with a new flexibility in leadership, likening this to the life of a stream. She speaks poetically of 'the water's need to flow':

> Water answers to gravity, to downhill, to the call of ocean. The form changes, but the mission remains clear. Structures emerge, but only as temporary solutions that facilitate rather than interfere. There is none of the rigid reliance that I have learned in organizations on single forms, on true answers and past practices. Streams have more than one response to rocks; otherwise there would be no Grand Canyon.

She suggests that there is a need for our organizational body to live with a new kind of faith, in a body that can accomplish its purpose in a variety of ways; what works best, however, is when a group of people 'focus on intent and vision, letting forms emerge and disappear'. She makes the point that such flexibility in decision-making and common purpose is powerfully established as an energy when it is generated by the relationships we seek to create with one another.[5]

As leaders we allow this 'flow' to happen as we welcome new folk into the community of love that should only ever have metaphorical walls. It's interesting that, as in programmes like the BBC 2 series *Rev*, we often talk with a mixture of warm affection and defensive ownership of this 'place' as 'my' church or parish. Parishioners also project this onto us with the same ambivalent feelings attached. When I announced to our congregation recently that I was soon to move on to a different role within our diocese, one parishioner said to me quite thoughtfully, 'Well, I guess we assume that we kind of own you, that you are ours completely.'

The Bible is full of individuals, and whole nations, who travel through life in fluidity. Jesus himself was a peripatetic, slightly nomadic figure living against the tide, possessing nothing. If anything, his ministry was to communicate his message, then pass on, his authority being, he knew, ultimately God's. His task was to inspire and make ready the disciples to be propagators of a message that was more powerful when spread and multiplied than any group of people or building. In Matthew 8.20 Jesus says, 'Foxes have holes, and birds of the air have nests; but the Son of Man has nowhere to lay his head.' Throughout his ministry he stays in a variety of other people's homes; even as he dies he is laid in a borrowed tomb. We tend to forget that a large percentage of the world's population do not own a home; they live wherever they can find shelter and safety. Many cultures understand the idea of 'ownership' much more loosely than from an individual perspective. Some people rent interior space all their lives, perhaps because they do not have the financial resources to own a property, or simply because the prevailing culture does not view individual home ownership as important.

The controversial graffiti artist Banksy 'borrows' public wall space to communicate often anti-establishment political and social statements through his art. He states that creating art in this way means that 'there is no elitism or hype, it [his art] exhibits on the best walls a town has to offer and nobody is put off by the price of admission'.[6] His work makes a powerful statement about how art, as well as politics, should be available for everyone, in contrast to the contemporary environment where art is sold for millions. In a different way, the environmental artist Andy Goldsworthy constructs organic works of art from a selection of materials from stone to straw, clay and ice. These are subject to natural change and decomposition as they are exposed to the elements that become part of their intrinsic beauty.

Understanding ourselves as people who experience and contribute and yet do not possess in a controlling way is surely an extension of the resurrection life of Jesus. In John 14, in the famous mystical passage often read at funerals, Jesus tells his disciples that he goes to prepare 'a place' for them. With characteristic dimness they don't understand, but what he is telling them is that this 'kingdom place' is not a physical place that can be grasped and claimed; it will be both everywhere and nowhere. And its results will be seen, touched and felt in real people and places – then as now – in what we call the Church. Thomas Merton talks about this in terms of paradoxical slavery and freedom:

> The free man is the one whose choices have given him the power to stand on his own feet and determine his own life according to the higher light and spirit that are in him. The slave, in the spiritual order, is the man whose choices have destroyed all spontaneity in him and have delivered him over, bound hand and foot, to his own compulsions, idiosyncrasies and illusions. He who is a slave is therefore never stable, never secure. He is always at the mercy of change. Therefore he cannot rest.[7]

Merton goes on to say, however, that blind renunciation of our own autonomy is not the answer, but that love must be at the heart of all freedom in living and in spirituality. But so often, he says, we do not trust in this freedom – the freedom of the unpredictable blowing of God's spirit, a potential source of a new way of living life – because we are too rooted in our own attachments.

Perhaps, then, there is a way of creating a theology of holy flux – a way of living our lives in and through faith that hangs loose to all things, people and situations we instinctively want to possess and see as 'ours'. As Timothy Radcliffe says, 'We are called to witness to a deeper freedom, which is to give our lives away, as Christ did.'[8] With this can come an understanding of living life in the power of the Spirit, which interprets how we live through a different lens. We create an outlook with an alternative consciousness, in a way that leaves a legacy but one that enjoys the fluidity of non-possessiveness. In a wonderful passage about the experience of moving house, Malcolm Boyd describes leaving his home, a time when trauma and new opportunity are powerfully juxtaposed:

> I suddenly realised this was my home, *my home*. It was time to go, but I hadn't even left my mark on it – not a mark. Yet what mark could I have left there but my breath on the walls, my footsteps on the floors, and my life in the rooms? And had I not been given something to take away with me and puzzle over, this easy-going informal community amid anonymity? There were possibilities for sharing with others that I had let slip because I felt both attracted and threatened. It's moving day again: an opportunity for new people, new choices.[9]

Christians, perhaps more than anyone, 'should be ruthless and radical towards the possessive instinct in themselves', in the words of John Dalrymple, always aware of the unending spiral of personal desire that has the capacity to overthrow the needs of both our local and global brothers and sisters. The first two commandments, he says, contain everything for the potential development of an attitude of detachment from self and stuff that is not compatible with an acquisitive spirit. He says this: 'The surrender to God in adoration and to one's neighbour in availability imply a "letting go" which is the opposite of the acquisitive "hanging on".'[10] The lines by Annie Dillard at the beginning of the chapter are this scientist's musing on the flexibility of mangrove plants that are for her 'artists of the beautiful, floating islands that are loose, alive and homeless on the water'.[11] She uses this to reflect on humanity's adaptability as sojourners, as well as on the underlying anxiety that we often remain unsure of where we actually belong. She continues her thinking on the word 'sojourners' which, she says, 'invokes a nomadic people's sense of vagrancy, a praying people's knowledge of estrangement, a thinking people's intuition of sharp loss'. In many ways we will never have 'space' enough – we will always want more, with our yearning to possess that will never truly be satisfied, yet our days on the earth are as a shadow. On a global level this is about us as Christian people developing an ongoing, renewed sense of loving respect for the earth and what it produces for our benefit. We are always only ever travellers who must tread lightly in the name of good stewardship, both for ourselves and for future generations.

In his book *The Cowshed Revolution*, Ray Simpson advocates a championing of the idea of downward mobility – in essence the conscious choice of living that sacrificially lays down life for the common good. Simpson explores, with a new vitality, stories of biblical precedents and saints from past and present who have attempted to live out their faith with conscious methods of non-possession and flexibility. Aidan and Chad, the planters of Celtic Christianity, politely refused the offer of King Oswald's horse, choosing instead to walk round the lands of the north to spread the news of the kingdom of God. The last section of Simpson's book contains examples of successful alternative economic schemes and social projects with a downwardly mobile and more fluid way of trading and treating others. Examples of this type of enterprise might include the recent enthusiasm for various forms of credit unions, or small projects where professional people give up a percentage of their paid working time, or even their homes, to welcome and care for those who are needier then they are. The Narthex, in Sparkhill in Birmingham, is one such project. Geoff and Joy Holt moved out of their home in the leafy suburbs to buy a larger residence in the urban priority area of Sparkhill where 90 per cent of the population are Muslim. The house now provides a haven and resource centre for a variety of multiracial projects, from child and health care to residency and homelessness issues, while on Sundays those in need, including asylum seekers, share meals together.

The life of God within us is given principally as gift. Like a stream that flows continuously from a high mountain here is an energy that is always available to quench our thirst for God and give us life, but it is an energy too that can never be contained or stopped. Such energy, in whatever form, is always freely in a state of flux, available to all who seek and need it. In this way our faith can engender an approach to life that creates a spirit of loving non-possession of anything and everything, from the concepts of home and friendship to the areas of work and communities we have responsibility for. Flux is about allowing ourselves and our souls to move with the life of God's spirit within as well as without; it is about us retaining the ability to see both sides of the argument, about giving ourselves permission to change our minds and to release others from the tight hold we might have on them. Flux can demonstrate a renewed openness to every aspect of our lives. The Romanian theologian Dumitru Stăniloae has stated that this is about offering something of this gift back to God, in blessing and gratitude, thus letting go of the idea that any created thing exists solely for our use (or abuse).[12]

The Methodist Covenant prayer, said together by members of the Methodist community at the beginning of each year, is a profound statement of non-possessiveness and anti-covetousness. Resonating with the sentiments of Ecclesiastes 3 and other Christian prayers, it takes up the idea that even our own lives should be understood as vessels that are created for the overriding glory of God. We are to live our lives in consummate trust, believing that our bodies, our wills and hearts are phenomena through which the power and life of God can move and change us, directing our course and strengthening our desire to work for the good of others. The natural balance of the prayer protects humanity from a dangerous denigration of 'the self', for the words speak not only of being 'empty, of being brought low and of having nothing' but also of 'being full' and 'exalted', of having 'all things'. Here in essence is a theology and a spiritualty with peaks and troughs, which abandons itself to the consecrated flux and flow of the loving force of the living God.

> I am no longer my own but yours.
> Put me to what you will,
> Rank me with whom you will;
> Put me to doing, put me to suffering;
> Let me be employed for you or laid aside for you,
> Exalted for you or brought low for you.
> Let me be full, let me be empty,
> Let me have all things, let me have nothing.
> I freely and wholeheartedly yield all things
> To your pleasure and disposal.
> And now, glorious and blessed God,
> Father, Son and Holy Spirit,
> You are mine and I am yours.
> So be it.
> And the covenant made on earth,
> Let it be ratified in heaven.
> Amen.[13]

Flux in practice

Individual

- Read any gospel stories where people undergo a significant change of heart or find themselves in a sudden new situation – the Prodigal Son or Zacchaeus, Mary in the birth narratives, Peter as he accepts the servanthood of Jesus. Reflect on their attitude and how these individuals became greater people through their ability to be fluid and open to the life of God.
- Reflect on your own attitude to possession, whether this is a project you manage, material things or people you might be overly controlling of at times. Think through how you could provide more freedom for someone else to blossom, or take on a new role or responsibility; or just how you might enable others to be themselves. Think about something physical you could share or let go of more.
- Reflect on how you might be 'set in your ways', either in attitude or through habit. Think about how you might become more open to another perspective or how you might understand a situation through new study or by talking to someone with a very different experience of life. Give yourself permission to be changed.

Corporate

- Encourage a healthy attitude to change but manage this prayerfully and carefully (which often means, in church life, slowly and patiently). The concept of flux is itself biblical and can be threaded through sermons and reflections, perhaps becoming the subject of study and group material. Studying the physical journeys individuals and peoples take in the Bible and how they are changed can be illuminating, from the Israelites as they are led into the Promised Land by Moses, to Joseph as he is captured and taken to Egypt, to

Ruth and Naomi who travel to return to their homeland. They can help us to discern how God acts through experience of sudden crisis and unpredictable change, and perhaps to make links with what may be happening in church life now.

- If you preach or lead groups regularly, try presenting both sides of an argument if appropriate.
- Encourage an attitude of 'our' church being for everyone rather than just for 'us'. How could your building be used more flexibly or for community use?
- Construct a service that helps people to live less materialistically in small and manageable ways.

4

Dark

Containing and confronting the difficult

———◆·◎·◆———

I don't find happiness a particularly interesting subject. My stories tend to be bittersweet because relationships aren't light and frivolous – they are the most dramatic and painful things that happen to us. (David Nicholls)

The future is by definition the unsayable and the uncontrollable, filled with paradoxes, mysteries, and confusions. It is an imperfect world at every level. Therefore the future is always, somehow, scary. (Richard Rohr, *The Naked Now*)[1]

Chris Gollon's 2014 exhibition at Guildford Cathedral showed an image of Mary the mother of Jesus seated, the dead Christ laid in her lap. The viewer is a witness of the aftermath of this both personal and global horror, and it feels as though we see straight into a mother's numbed soul. Mary's haunted eyes stare out; her gaze is beyond us, her hands imploring something, somewhere. She sits wrapped in a voluminous dark robe where the pietà is laid out. Here in this moment, she seems cloaked in heaviness as she too becomes the recipient of the darkness that has murdered her son. Yet her face and her praying, pleading hands are lit up with chiaroscuro, as is the limp body of Jesus. In this darkness, the light has not quite evaporated.

As clergy we are often containers and carriers of 'the dark' – dark meaning the agonies that happen to us and to those we attempt to care for. Dark is the monotonous melancholy that so many people carry within them. Dark is everything from the painful memory of broken things in our lives to the elements beyond our control that we assume control our happiness. And it is the unending and unimaginable evil that beheads innocent aid workers and guns down the young – things that seem inconceivable to reasonable people like ourselves. Dark is personal and colluding sin, it is lack of love, it is the result of long-term illness or strain. Dark is the struggle that narrows the borders of our existence. As priests we cannot help others face their dark if we have not faced our own; facing our darkness is an ongoing and courageous conversation about the depths of our nature as human people, both individually and collectively. It is especially costly to be experiencing a period of dark when you are trying to help others, but this can make us more authentic than we might have been otherwise, ironically helping rather than hindering others – it is Henri Nouwen's 'wounded healer'.

Most people have an innate desire to help others, to be a step on a journey to ease, to soothe or to break free from the vicious circle. It's true of our profession too. Jesus comes to free us from whatever well we fall into, and helps us to see that the gift of the life of God has already been given to us. But mostly it is not as simple as this, for darkness has the frightening propensity to coat our freedom, refusing to be easily dispensed with. Leaders need to be unafraid to name their personal demons, and also to be ready to enable other people to face theirs, if this is the challenge they bring to us.

It is hard to look at what is dark, just as it is difficult to look at what is truly bright and to realize that in fact we need the darkness in order to appreciate the luminance of the stars. The tortured sculpture of *Christ Crucified* by Brazilian artist Guido Rocha, produced in 1979, is not easy for any compassionate person to look at. It is atrocious in its overtones of the dark affliction that human beings can impose upon each other and upon God himself. In a similar way we find it uncomfortable to study our own and others' darkness, to delve and discover

54

what we are ashamed of, distressed with, or both. This is why we wear masks of normality, most of the time. One church member, whose recent darkness was revealed to me as priest, has stopped coming to church because, he says, he feels as though that darkness is no longer contained and internal, and that everyone can see his agitated heart and exposed soul. The Afghan-American writer Khaled Hosseini, in his beautifully crafted novel *And the Mountains Echoed*, describes a character whose face has been badly mauled by a dog. There is a moment when she is given permission by her aunt to dispense with the mask for ever:

> For a long time Thalia didn't make a move or say a word. Then, slowly, her hands rose, and she untied the mask. I looked at her directly in the face. I felt an involuntary urge to recoil, the way you would at a sudden loud noise. But I didn't. I held my gaze.[2]

But as in a solar eclipse, faith tells us that there is always light behind such darkness. The word 'eclipse' means abandonment, or the darkening of a heavenly body. For people of faith this is how life can feel, when we are suffocated with the genuine hardness or pain of a bereavement, a shock, or an ongoing situation of relentlessness. But as people of hope we believe that the light is there even if we ourselves are struggling to see it. As Christian leaders we can be there, struggling to break through people's darkness, if that is what they need us to do. In 2010, part of a copper-gold mine in the Atacama desert in Chile caved in, trapping 33 men 700 metres underground and 500 metres from the mine's entrance. After 69 days all 33 were brought safely to the surface, almost all in good medical condition. Part of priesthood is gently, carefully mining the depths within others when this is needed, and also letting those who are struggling in their darkness know that there are people who are prepared to work hard for 'release', people who can offer spiritual guidance and biblical hope. What enabled the miners to retain hope was the knowledge that while they were trapped internally in the depths of the earth, others were struggling above ground to free them, and were doing so carefully in order to avoid any further collapse. But until very near the end of the rescue the miners did not know whether it was going to be possible for them to be rescued at all. We are not God, but accompanying others through their darkness occasionally gives respite to the intensity of a dark experience. The power of God gives us the strength to step right into such a hinterland. It may give us permission, perhaps, to provide through a sacramental presence an opportunity to seek and speak the truth, within ourselves first and also in others.

Our calling as spiritual leaders today is to live both comfortably and uncomfortably with and in this 'dark' when we encounter it – to effectively be people who cope with mystery. We are already doing it – for example, in the 'not knowing' of what will happen in the long term to our Church and its various issues, in the thorny questions that divide its body; and in 'not knowing' the outcome of the multifarious pastoral issues people carry and bring to us. And what connects all these is our accompanying others in their confusion, in their 'not knowing' where God is, and in the frustrated shadows of either not having or not understanding the answers. We feel the pressure to present certainties to those living with dark, to speak and behave as religious experts, rather than as people who are captivated by a vision of an expansive love we feel compelled to share whatever we are experiencing. A wonderful story comes from a current candidate for ordination who works with a Fresh Expressions project in central Chester. 'Night Church' runs on Saturday nights from 9.30 p.m. until 2 a.m., and offers hospitable physical and spiritual sanctuary for those out and about in the bars, clubs and streets of the city – people who need a temporary haven for whatever reason. Gill tells the story of a man who wandered in, describing himself as an atheist, but nevertheless went to the front and lit a candle. Clearly moved by the experience of coming into a dark church full of candles the man began to talk, expressing his past discomfort with the 'things of church and people of Christian faith'. Gill describes their conversation as going a little like this.

> The man said, 'I am really glad that I came in here. It's really
> nice in here, isn't it?'
>
> 'Yes, it is,' I replied.
>
> 'It's really peaceful,' he said.
>
> 'Yes, I think so too,' I replied.
>
> 'I'm an atheist,' he offered, unprompted.
>
> 'Yes, your friend was telling me,' I said.
>
> 'I lead funerals, humanist funerals,' he said. After a pause he
> continued, 'I really like it in here, though, but I'm not religious.'
>
> 'I'm not really religious either,' I said.
>
> 'The problem with Christianity', he said, 'is that it tells you
> what you have to believe, it's all rules.'
>
> I smiled. 'I agree with you – if it is like that, then that's a
> problem because I don't think we can box God in. I think God
> is in so many ways beyond my understanding, and there is a
> mystery to faith. Perhaps,' I continued, 'you and I are not really
> as different as you might think. We are both on a journey of
> discovery of sorts.'
>
> He was quiet for a moment and then said, gazing up at the
> church, 'There is something, isn't there?'
>
> 'Yes, I think there is,' I replied. 'For me as a Christian I would
> say that the "something" is the God of the Bible.'
>
> He reached out and shook my hand. 'Thank you so much, it
> has been really lovely to come in here and meet you,' he said.
>
> 'You too,' I said, 'and God bless you.'
>
> 'And God bless you too,' he said, 'whoever this God is to you.'
>
> We both laughed, and with that he left to catch up with his
> friends.

Gill, who has an instinctive ability to allow someone to feel
their way through the workings of God's Spirit, simply allowed
this person to express some of his past hurt and discomfort.
She responded to whatever he spoke or asked about, in gentle-
ness. The dark, if we are able to stand within it, can be powerful
beyond measure. Here, the evident intertwining of physical
darkness and light (a dark but open church, and the presence

of an open and unthreatened Christian person) proved the catalyst to a *kairos* moment for one individual.

This is where the profound theology of St John of the Cross has much to say to a twenty-first-century tangled consciousness which tends to feel more comfortable in the assured certainties of secular rationalization and scientific proof. But such a consciousness is also often strangely drawn to an ancient sense that 'unknowing' can, in fact, be lived in and with. In *The Naked Now: Learning to See as the Mystics See*, the Franciscan priest Richard Rohr suggests that modern educational methods and spiritual approaches are too one-dimensional. The Church, for one, no longer teaches those searching for answers or personal transformation how to be mystical, how to look for layers in an interpretation of life experience. He describes this as looking at our lives in a certain way, akin to tuning into the right frequencies on a radio, so that we can pick up the signal of God which underlies everything in a life lived out in faith. Unpacked, this is about human beings experiencing life (he uses the example of looking at a sunset) on three potential levels – physical appreciation of beauty and wonder, scientific understanding, and finally a level where the underlying mystery that connects the individual with something greater can be sensed. While the first two are important, it is in the third way that the mystical person experiences life, moving away from mere mental belief to see and feel God's presence both within and without us.

But articulating God remains a part of darkness for both ancient and contemporary mystics, as identified by the author of the fourteenth-century mystical text *The Cloud of Unknowing*. When we get to the third stage described above we sense that there is something dark and mysterious always between ourselves and God.

> This darkness and cloud is always between you and your God, no matter what you do, and it prevents you from seeing him clearly by the light of understanding in your reason ... So set

yourself to rest in this darkness as long as you can, always crying out after him whom you love.[3]

Within the mystical tradition is the recognition that humans will intuitively sense the presence of God beyond pain, beauty and reason, but we will never have the full capacity to articulate it completely either. Perhaps this is particularly true of times when we experience the dark at a deep level ourselves.

One thing that hits people like a stone wall if they go far enough along this inner journey is the anxious vacancy of unbelief – the possibility that in fact God does not exist, is temporarily absent, or cannot be retrieved from a previous life of faith. Such experiences often run simultaneously alongside the feeling that they have somehow failed in their spiritual efforts. For St John of the Cross, the sixteenth-century Carmelite friar and mystic, this forms part of the 'dark night' experience. As Helen Marshall puts it, 'night' might come to us in recognizable forms – unemployment, bereavement, rejection – but also in a sense of greyness, spiritual dryness and bewilderment, times moreover when we may seriously question whether God is a reality at all.[4] At such times we actually have no choice but to grasp at trust, even if it feels like catching dust. For dark mystics like St John, the sharpest spiritual reality is the belief that the soul makes the greatest progress when it travels in this dark, not knowing what will happen but becoming more and more aware of its own limitations and vulnerability. This pathway challenges those walking it to slowly dispense with everything the ego says we need and desire, including theological answers and physical certainties.

Dark in this sense is about having no choice but to rely on the mystery that is love – love that leads us into the dark, through it and ultimately out of it. Olive Wyon reworks some of this, which can seem rather arcane to the contemporary mind:

In such darkness there is nothing to fear. Often we feel as though we were travelling in the wrong direction; but by faith we know that we are not alone; that God is with us, leading and sustaining us all the time. Gradually, as we learn to adjust ourselves to this new way of living, we begin to understand why God must work in this secret way: he has to do so, because if we could see what he was doing we might become far too interested in the process, and then we would spoil his work by looking at ourselves instead of at him. All we are asked to do is to keep moving: 'Some run swiftly; some walk; some creep painfully; but everyone who keeps on will reach the goal.'[5]

St John talks about two kinds of 'night' – the 'night of the senses', which makes us loosen our grip on material things, and the 'night of the spirit', where spiritual certainties slip from our grasp as well. In terms of the latter this is about us learning to trust, to push forwards through the darkness even when we have no sense of belief in God's presence – a testing calling. The deepest and perhaps most harrowing experience of this darkness might be the more passive, when we have no choice but to allow God's grace to work within us in ways we cannot comprehend at the time we are living through them. As priest I have sometimes walked alongside those who desperately want faith, but it remains unattainable or slips from their grasp because that person has borne the brunt of life's hardships and cannot reconcile this with belief in God. For those who are the accompaniers such a journey sometimes takes its toll in terms of a subtle inner whisper of doubt as well.

But the reality for most of us as our faith matures is that we begin to see more of our own darkness rather than less. So we become increasingly aware of our self-obsession, our fragility, our selfishness, our unresolved bitterness, our disguised profanity. And rather than feeling that we know more and more clearly who God is, maybe we are happier in unknowing and in the undogmatic. Good priests understand this very well – it is the continual work of God's Holy Spirit wrestling within us. It is also perhaps the cultivation of a divine humility, accepting that it is indeed hard to describe and pin down the person of God. At times this might feel frustrating, as we sense it is a kind of 'one step forward, two steps back' situation, but in fact the more we let go of our selves and our apparent competencies, the more God remodels us – like a holy sculptor, shaping us into beautiful beings. We can bring to those we serve encouragement in their dark when we live in this prayerful journey ourselves.

What we have to remember to tell others (both those of faith and of none) when they come to us with their dark dimensions is that ironically, even though it might not feel like it, such an experience can be positive, as well as a mature part of faith 'growing up'. It is easy to experience God's presence when life is rosy and sweet, when all is well, peaceful and harmonious. And at these times it is important we express gratitude and feel the joy. But our faith remains shallow and saccharin when it cannot cope with the diamond-hard questions of unbelief, and confront the voiceless struggle of Jesus writing in the dust as well as his anguished cry from the cross: 'My God, my God, why have you forsaken me?' Helen Marshall writes: 'To yearn after God in the bleakest, darkest and most desolating experiences of faith is to identify with Christ, and his Spirit is formed within us.'[6] St John of the Cross says that because Jesus has gone through this himself, the dark journey is one of hope rather than desperation. But at times it is about dispensing with something that is stopping us being free, preventing us from being more expansive as people.

The film *127 Hours* tells the true story of Aron Ralston, who in 2003 fell into a slot canyon while mountain biking, miles from home, in the Utah desert. As he fell, a huge boulder fell with him, entirely trapping his right forearm. After five days Aron made the courageous decision to amputate his arm, using a blunt penknife, in order to save his life and gain his freedom. The film is based on Ralston's autobiography, *127 Hours: Between a Rock and a Hard Place.*[7] He makes this momentous decision to literally sever a part of himself in order to save his life. The film plays with the glare of sunlight juxtaposed with the shadowed evening, symbolizing his grappling with the darkness of amputation, fluctuating between believing he is capable of such an act and feeling that the task is too great. Eventually, after suffering heat, dehydration and loneliness, Ralston set himself free, leaving a part of himself behind in that dark chasm. Interviewed after the experience, he describes the journey to that point in spiritual terms, as he begins to see a vision of his future son, as yet unborn.

> The vision absolutely showed me that I was not going to die in the canyon. And it was a powerful experience that came at a time when I believed I was going to die that night. I was convinced of it ... There's some very deep energies that we occasionally tap into, kind of lifting the veil of what's underneath all of this. But it takes a lot of sometimes extreme circumstances of life or death to get to that point of where all the day to day stuff gets stripped away and you get to that core that's behind the mist.

What Ralston is describing is essentially a spiritual experience, one where he realized he had to make a choice whether to live or die. Penetrating the darkness, reaching the bottom of it and ultimately moving beyond it, he found the chink that was his exit – hope and life.

Carmelite nun Constance Fitzgerald suggests that the dark night can be potentially relevant to any situation of impasse in our lives. 'By impasse, I mean that there is no way out, no way round, no rational escape from what imprisons one, no possibilities in the situation.'[8] We find ourselves in a place of utter powerlessness and the temptation is to just give up, particularly on God and faith. But St John encourages us to trust the feeling, to see the light in new possibilities. The question many would ask is 'Why?' Why on earth do we go through this? What is the point, particularly when the God we believe in is a God of light and ever-present love rather than darkness and absence? This is a highly relevant, contemporary puzzlement from a society that is not prepared to understand the concept of unnecessary sacrifice. Voluntary darkness feels like self-flagellation, astringent and irrelevant.

In *Letters from the Desert*, Carlo Carretto describes how the dark sky is necessary in order to see the sharp illumination of the stars.

> I felt as if I were wrapped around by the blanket of the friendly night, a blanket embroidered with stars. When my faith was weak, all this would have seemed incomprehensible to me. I was afraid as a child is of the night. The night is no longer my enemy, nor does it make me afraid. On the contrary, its darkness and divine transcendence are a source of delight. The darkness is necessary, the darkness of faith is necessary, for God's light is too great. It wounds. I understand more and more that faith is not a mysterious and cruel trick of a God who hides himself without telling me why, but a necessary veil. My discovery of him takes place gradually, respecting the growth of divine life in me.[9]

In other words, we need the blackness of the night sky in order to understand what and where the stars are. Not shying away from the idea that the mystery of God can evolve and gradually unfold throughout our lives can, strangely, make sense to people in our pastoral care. But perhaps many of us do not sit comfortably with mystery and unknowing, thirsting after an antidote to the insecurity of modern life. But the dark night is naked and real and we can go places from its depths. By understanding that God *is* in this place we are also strengthened to resist the urge to be pulled into the deeper darkness of evil.

Clergy can also help those they lead to face darkness, when such darkness symbolizes evil, and this forms another way of living a prayerful life. This is the dark confrontation of facing the inherent evil in the world but which also manifests itself within ourselves. Jim Thompson, in *Stepney Calling: Thoughts for our Day*, says: 'We do not have to travel far to explore the reality of evil because it can and should be studied in the battlefield of our own mind. If we find it there, we can be sure that in the affairs of society, in the great affairs of the nations, it will be rampant.'[10] As we become spiritually mature, the stronger our sensitivity to evil becomes as we embark upon battles that at times feel immense. We also need to be people who can name evil. Rowan Williams has asked whether in an increasingly secular environment we have an adequate vocabulary to name and speak about such a darkness. He writes:

> Evil becomes a trivially emotive way of referring to what we hate or fear or just disapprove of, rather than a word which describes an inherent and unavoidable part of who we are, the inevitable result of the fact that our world, however we might choose to describe it, is 'fallen' and that human beings are capable of the most astonishing violence and weakness of sturdy and loving morality.[11]

Confronting evil is hard at any level. Real, horrendous, excruciating evil that makes us wince internally, as our minds grapple with how some things can actually be possible, can be difficult to deal with. These days, if we have any loving awareness of others, we can easily feel 'compassion overload' and sometimes wonder what we can do to ease situations of horror (particularly in areas geographically far away). Janet Morley, commenting on a poem by Margaret Atwood, 'It is dangerous to read newspapers', in her book *A Heart's Time*, describes this position perfectly. Never before has news from around the world become so easily accessible, through the internet, newspapers and television, as we are reminded vividly of the details of human cruelty and suffering taking place in the same world as we are living in. 'We are left without a resolution, uncomfortably reflecting on what our own responsibilities are, in this continually sinful and violent world.'[12] We cannot do everything – perhaps we feel we cannot actually do very much at all – but what is crucial is that we *do something*; we need to summon the courage to confront some imperfect and evil situation in our world that is causing current human suffering. This is part of our faithfulness and responsibility as Christians, and especially as leaders, however uncomfortable this feels at times. In my experience people respond to becoming involved in 'acts of justice', for want of a better word; they would like to feel that what they do and how they pray is making a tangible difference to someone, somewhere. Our moral framework is axiomatic to our faith and also provides an alternative starting point to the agenda of human rights so prevalent in the secular and humanist West. To do this together as Christian people is to retain the brave ability to look at our God who endured the terror of the cross and to see him in those suffering. It is interesting to reflect that the significance of Holy Week and attendance at its services are simultaneously diminishing in collective expressions of faith. Of late I have heard clergy colleagues bemoaning (with heartfelt distress) that so many folk seem to 'skip' the emotional journey that Holy Week asks us to participate in, arriving at the joy of Easter without having faced the pain of God. But mature faith tells us that we cannot have Easter without Good Friday; we cannot understand light without knowing what dark is, or understand joy if we have not at least grappled with pain. Confronting the darkness of evil can be supported by theodicy – the belief that God is good and justice will overcome all ultimately in the face of evil. This is about facing the evil as hopeful people who believe that even the smallest prayer and actions change things.

But all this comes at a cost and the mystics understood this too. A few years ago I got involved in a charity that helped provide protection, education and love for street children in the city of Medellín, Colombia. Our youth group lived out on the streets of our town for 24 hours, and we arranged a street collection raising thousands of pounds. The coordinator of the charity came to speak to our churches on several occasions, often sharing distressing details of what was happening to the children, some as young as six, at the time the age of my own son. The work spiralled, expanding to include an annual ecumenical financial collection with awareness raising at harvest time. All good Christian stuff, but I was aware that I was beginning to find the work costly in terms of over-empathizing with the situation. When we face evil straight in the face and are drawn in, allowing ourselves to get internally involved, it is costly and Christ-like. To attempt to love the perpetrators of evil and those who behave abhorrently is itself a subversive yet potentially transformative act.

For many, facing such evil comes at tremendous cost and occasionally proves too great. We must guard our hearts and our mental health to a certain extent, but by stepping into such darkness we have the chance to ease others' pain and stand up against the same evil Jesus himself confronted and challenged. The film *Oranges and Sunshine* (2010) is the true story of a Nottingham social worker, Margaret Humphreys, who accidentally discovered the scandalous deportation of thousands of children from poor backgrounds from Britain to Australia in the 1950s and 1960s. This became an all-consuming and costly emotional journey for her. At one point in the film, after a visit to the remote children's home with a former deportee, she breaks down. Len, one of the former children, says, 'Margaret, you carry so much of this pain for all of us just when we can't do it any more.' This is a deeply sacrificial ministry – one that steps right into the evil of the past and the present lingering consequences.

Facing the dark in this way is costly but it is part of living a prayerful life that takes the evil of the world seriously while allowing ourselves to absorb (even just a little) some of its results. Facing the dark means that we reflect on our own capacity to do harm, not in an introspective, guilt-inducing way, but because we are inevitably part of a bigger whole. Facing the dark is about prophetically seeing beyond what seems obvious and that which appears to be acceptable and naming what is damaging and starkly wrong in our personal lives, in our churches and in the world. It is about modelling an offering that allows our own hearts to share the pain of others but refuses to offer unhelpful platitudes. Facing the dark is a gutsy and courageous part of our spirituality that is about risk and silence, about radical love and healing scars, about making a difference with the power of the Spirit.

Dark in practice

Individual

- If you are experiencing a time of spiritual darkness (including uncertainty about God's existence), do not agonize over this. Do not worry about 'believing'. Try not to allow what are primarily cerebral thoughts to harden to become scepticism or negativity. Try to stay in the darkness and live with the state of being that can understand the questions and doubts as a spiritual experience in themselves. This may not feel very natural in a faith environment that often demands that we 'believe' things rather than experience them but when we are living through a sense of darkness it can be much more helpful to concentrate on where the gifts are in our life, and where we find and experience love.
- Regularly take time to look within yourself to try to identify where your own dark parts are. This should never become a navel-gazing, guilt-inducing exercise where we end up feeling we are bad people or failed disciples. The Psalms can be read as prayers that express the full range of human emotions in honesty and passion, prayers that struggle with the whole gamut of human despair and elevation in terms of how humanity operates and how God can feel both present and absent. Always pray in the knowledge that we are deeply and completely loved, whatever we have done or might do in the future and however much we might think we fall short of

being a follower of Jesus. As Acts 17.28 says, 'In him we live and move and have our being.' But it can be productive to gently challenge our inner 'dark' parts – those things that might not be considered traditional 'sins' but can halt our blossoming into the people God wants us to be. Our dark parts are the things that can clip our wings, continuously obstruct transformation and stop us living in freedom and trust. For me it can be a constant anxiety over money, my judgement of others, my anger, the scars from my past. As you honestly look at these, pray that God will change you. Sing the Taizé chant, 'Spirit of the Living God, fall afresh on me'.

- Use the newspaper or other kind of daily news to pray about and through evil and dark situations, believing as you do so that through your efforts God takes your prayers and uses them to ease someone's situation.

Corporate

- Encourage your congregation to attend to Holy Week seriously and explain why it is important to do this as disciples. If you don't have many additional Holy Week services, consider introducing just one more.
- If you don't already, identify a problematic situation in the world, or in your own local community, and pray for it. See what social action you can get involved in connected with this. Listen to your congregation to find out whether anyone has an interest or knowledge about a particular issue. Just one 'ministry' in this way is powerful as well as manageable, and can counterbalance the feeling of being overwhelmed by a violent world.
- Lead an evening service that focuses on the mystical tradition, or lead a study group looking at the theology of St John of the Cross, Meister Eckhart, *The Cloud of Unknowing* and Gregory of Nyssa – all proponents of this approach to the divine at different times and places.

5

Stretch

Stepping out of our comfort zone

———◆———

Authentic Christian living, either individually or as a community, reaches out for more, because Christianity is a social religion, and it has a sting. Jesus was a teacher and a healer but his message had a revolutionary thrust. If he had simply taught about the way to achieve serenity he would hardly have been worth crucifying.   (John Pritchard, *The Life and Work of a Priest*)

The wind can be blowing, but if your sail isn't raised, you won't go far.   (Brian McLaren, *We Make the Road by Walking*)[1]

A few years ago a fit friend persuaded me to compete in a local triathlon. Never considering myself a sporty person, this felt something of a challenge, definitely taking me out of my physical comfort zone. I trained hard in a multidisciplinary way, feeling my body undergoing pain in the development of muscles it was not used to using, as well as gradually getting fitter, stronger and mentally better, through the pushing of my own limits. The event consisted of 16 lengths in a swimming pool (tame for serious triathletes, perhaps), 15 miles of cycling, concluding with a three-and-a-half-mile run. In the end I achieved a time of just over two hours for the lot; although I came fairly near the bottom of the several hundred taking part, a feeling of intense pride rose up every time a parishioner mentioned the race.

It remains a very distinctive part of our human experience to challenge ourselves, sometimes to the limits of our physical, emotional and even spiritual existence. If we are people who think deeply about life, faith or both then these things can combine. It's true that some people naturally relish 'the challenge' and are always looking for it, their boredom levels never satisfied until the next itch is scratched or their thirst quenched. I might describe myself as a spiritual adrenalin junkie, loving a challenge, a new project (even a small one) both for myself and also as a potential journey to lead others into as well. This chapter discusses what might be described as the stretching that happens when people of faith *voluntarily* undertake challenge – large or small – and reflects on this in terms of physical as well as spiritual living through concepts such as pilgrimage where these two aspects merge and interact simultaneously.

It's clear that we can be inspired by people who do big, heart-stretching, mind-blowing things to expand the limits of human existence. On 14 October 2012 Felix Baumgartner jumped to earth from 120,000 feet in a climate-controlled capsule attached to a balloon, travelling faster than the speed of sound. We cannot but be wowed by such record-breaking. Television documentaries showing social experiments are popular, with ourselves as viewers observing ordinary people being pushed to their own limits. The Channel 4 programme *The Island*, overseen by the adventurer Bear Grylls, took 13 men out of their comfort zone and on to a remote Fijian island to see whether they were able to survive. Grylls watched and waited to see whether the pure essence of masculinity could emerge to do the hunter-gathering in seriously hot and uncomfortable conditions. Inevitably as the physical challenges unfolded they were discovered to contain what amounted to spiritual searching for some of the men, with inner questions of worth and inclusion rising to the surface. As Christians, we are particularly moved when people undertake a challenging act for God, perhaps especially when the point is to bring to light some kind of injustice in our world. Keith Hebden, Assistant Curate in Nottingham Diocese, seriously fasted for 40 days (on a diet of fruit juice and water) to support the launch of the End Hunger Fast campaign in 2014, highlighting to the government and others the scandal of food poverty in Britain at this time.

Even if we know we couldn't possible 'go there', stories of others 'stretching' themselves often become topics of conversations that we then share with other people, with our congregations (for those of us who lead), to illustrate the possibilities of what can be achieved to evangelize or to extract what is the essence and nature of the kingdom. Perhaps the stretching we are most uncomfortable with is that which happens when the challenge is emotional; mostly this happens in spite of us, when we have to cope with unforeseen and negative experiences. The death of someone we love, when illness or loss happens, often prompts difficult questions to rise to the forefront of our lives – 'How will I cope?' and 'Where is God in all the mess?'

But the first question we need to ask ourselves is 'Why?' Why do we want to, why should we look to be stretched, as humans and as Christians? For leaders it's about wanting those who sit in the pews each week to know that there is something they can do to feel like they are acting as people of faith. This is not to assume patronizingly that folk aren't already doing plenty for the kingdom; it is more about retaining an awareness that as God's gathered people this is an essential strand to our lived-out faith. It is an ever-present reminder that our calling is to place ourselves at the heart of those places and events where, because they are too dark or mercurial, others refuse to go. In recent months the West has been shocked by brutal murders of individuals such as Alan Henning, a taxi driver from Greater Manchester who was taken hostage and then beheaded; he had been travelling to Syria with humanitarian aid convoys to help the plight of refugees he never knew. Henning would not have anticipated the terrible fate that awaited him, but he would have known he was taking a risk; the point is that he was willing to go very much out of his comfort zone to respond to a globally appalling situation.

Most of us will never live out such a grave calling, but I have noticed that people respond to the idea of stretching – relishing, for example, the invitation to take up the 40 Lent challenges our church suggested as a way to mark the season in 2014. But there is a danger that we might tire our folk with constant requests. I possess the urge to be a provocative preacher, and one of my congregation said to me wearily after a Sunday sermon, 'Does everything always have to be such a *challenge*?' Another said with a smile, 'You never let us rest, do you?' It rang slight warning bells with me; our leadership needs to be mindful that we do not add to the load on our people, many of whom are already carrying much. There needs to be an awareness of the limits of our often elderly congregations who feel they have done 'all that' and now simply want to take a back seat. We should try to energize but not exhaust, allowing people to leave worship without feeling guilty that they are not doing enough or incapacitated because they are at a loss to know what to do to make a difference within the limits of their lives.

But on reflection, my silent answer to that comment on my sermon was 'Yes'. Yes, we are called to be challenged because the world needs people who are inspiring and admired for big humanity-stretching experiences, particularly spiritual ones. We need to stretch ourselves because then we become true witnesses to our capacity to love, through the power of God. Rowan Williams connects this with the idea of vocation:

> A 'vocation' isn't some weird and unusual thing; it's just the way in which we (all of us) recognize all this. God wants to move us on towards reality, honesty and fullness of life; and from time to time, we get a deepened sense of how he's at work and where he's inviting us to discover this. It doesn't take long to realize that these invitations are likely to take us well beyond our comfort zones – just because we're all of us used to seeing less of ourselves than is really there. We sense, somehow, that we're being prodded into territory that is strange and not at all

safe, even though we recognize at the same time that there's something about it that really matters to us and for us.[2]

Stretching was a large and vital part of the ministry of Jesus – he stretched himself, and others, in myriad ways. So choosing to stretch, to flex our spiritual muscles, is about becoming more Christ-like, and in doing so we follow in the footsteps of many a saint and disciple who have walked before us. We, like Jesus, can push the boundaries of the comfortable complacency in order to be an antidote to the acedia and lethargy in our society.

For Jesus, challenge was part of the call of the kingdom; it was unavoidable. Jesus invited those he came into contact with to stretch for a variety of reasons. Often it was a test of faith, both for themselves and for him. The stepping out from the boat on the water is the archetypal request (modelled first by Peter) to trust in what seems hard and impossible; the 'boat' symbolizes an environment of safety, be it emotional, physical or spiritual. Jesus asks us to step out and into something that is unknown, maybe even crazy or improbable – like the idea that we can walk on water towards God. Jesus asked people to dispense with their tightly held wealth, their tightly controlled religious and political opinions, and instead to walk into a whole new understanding of what life fulfilment is all about. The folk who encountered him were stretched, quizzed and sometimes singed. But stepping out of the boat reaps untold rewards, if we can do it with the power of the Holy Spirit flowing through our veins. With this mystical power we are all capable of a great deal, even when we do what we consider to be just something 'small'.

In Matthew 14 fear was the overriding emotion felt by the disciples, partly because of the storm, their boat battered by the waves and far from land. Fear meant that they clung to the familiar and safe space their boat had become. For many of us life is 'safe', as well as extremely comfortable in comparison to millions on the planet; most of us have homes of some description and financial resources to survive, often with a high standard of living. I recognize in my own life the tendency to create environments, friendship groups and work situations that feel safe. This usually means being surrounded by people who love me or know me well or who share 'the faith'. We all need such places of comfort but it's too easy to become so confined by an anaesthetized safety that we never move out to do things that might shatter our complacency, that might rock our worlds. Faith asks questions of us in this way – continually – urging us to consider going to the uncomfortable place, wherever this might be.

I write for ordinary Christians in the ordinary towns and cities of this country. So most of the time such stepping out can be very simple. On Maundy Thursday this year a group of us – myself and three colleagues – chose to do a voluntary shoe-shine for two hours in the main precinct of our town. The day was cold and windy, and people were very reluctant to stop and sit down to have their shoes cleaned. Shoppers have become used to this street being patrolled by charity workers, so it took some persuading that this was a simple offering of love – a contemporary form of foot-washing – something that honestly had no strings attached. There's a part of me that enjoys the stretching such 'public presence' brings, but on this day I heard a beguiling inner voice that told me I didn't have to 'get out of the boat'. On the street all ran smoothly, with enough encouraging encounters and recognition for this act of service to feel worthwhile, especially as a few brave members of the parish turned up to hand out leaflets and provide moral support. Afterwards the experience felt satisfying, as though we had got out of our comfort zones, if only in some minute way, and been faithful to Christ, witnessing something of the spirit of this momentous day, particularly through the genuinely open conversations we had with those who had engaged with us.

Timothy Radcliffe, while spending the month of May in Santa Sabina, Rome, relates the sight of young kestrels outside his window, trying desperately to stay airborne in the currents having been evicted from the comfortable safety of the nest by their parents and forced to fly. 'This is what the Holy Spirit does,' he says, '(if only we will let it), thrusting us out of our ecclesiastical nest into mission.' He muses on why it is that often, as followers of Jesus, we seem so reluctant to be *sent*. His answer is:

> Because it means dying to whom we have been ... We are sent on mission to discover who we are in and for those other people. The first mission of the Church to the Gentiles was the death to the Church's initial identity as a community that was solely Jewish.[3]

This was the early Church's first experience of setting something aside that felt deeply familiar and 'right', but was not to be the chosen way forward for God's moving and growing Church.

Part of good leadership is this gentle but continual encouragement to be stretched spiritually and to use our lives not only to set an example but to get this consciousness into the lifeblood of a church community's ministry. Open and conscientious clergy understand what it means to be stretched on God's behalf, for it often entails deliberately putting ourselves in places where we have no idea how people will respond to us, what we will do in a particular situation, or even whether we have the strength to do it. In *John Sentamu's Faith Stories*, Stuart Petty, an Anglican Chaplain at York District Hospital, writes:

> There's something important about being uncomfortable. When you get called onto a ward you don't know who you are going to meet. You get ushered behind a curtain and you have no idea of the dynamics, who these people are or what has happened. I've sat in an intensive care unit where actually there's nothing

to say, but it's important that I stay there. I had to learn that filling the silence was more my issue. It was about me being uncomfortable. Yet even when I can't think of anything to say, I'm amazed that God still finds a way to use me.[4]

Stretching must always have a point and that point must be a signpost that directs others to the living God. In 2010 the Christian writer Rhidian Brook took his wife and two children on a punchy journey through various parts of the world including Africa that have been particularly ravaged by AIDS. A friend had asked him to write a book researching the Salvation Army's response to the wreckage of HIV/AIDS around the world, and this led to what was a life-changing trip, along with the written record. In an article in *The Guardian*, Brook said:

> The decision to go was more about faith than reason. Reason said: what about malaria? What about the children missing school? What about lost work opportunities? And can you live without fresh milk on your muesli? Faith said: You can't see it yet but this could be a life-changing experience that you and the children will never forget.[5]

Through the writing of his book, *More Than Eyes Can See*, thousands of readers have been inspired. Interestingly he says this: 'I sometimes wondered if it was a good thing exposing my children to some of the things we encountered – the sickness, pain and loss caused by AIDS – but even the most uncomfortable situations seemed to have a redeeming quality.'[6] That comment came after a visit to a woman infected with the virus when Brook's son Gabriel slipped in some excrement and was understandably upset, being aged only nine. At a loss as to what to do next, the family witnessed the woman washing Gabriel's leg and shoe, using her only water supply, until he was entirely clean. This capacity for kindness despite her tragic circumstance became a life lesson that could only be experienced in such a situation.

Brook's comment about uncomfortable situations having redeeming potential takes us to the heart of faith, actually to the cross. It tells us simply why undertaking 'the stretch' becomes important and meaningful. Challenge for God, whether it's traipsing through a ravaged continent with your children or shoe-shining in a suburban high street, helps us to strengthen our own convictions in the power of a loving God, sometimes amid darkness or going against the grain of a learned complacency. It also helps others to understand how God's action is *alive* in the places they find themselves in. Brook says that he stopped looking for God in the darkest of situations because it soon dawned on him that God had already walked into them before him. Jesus says to Peter, 'Get out of your comfort zone and you will find me if you concentrate on trust as opposed to fearful wavering. Keep your eyes fixed on me and everything becomes possible, for I will fill you with power.'

The spiritual stretch requires a conscious effort and a decision to respond to the commands we hear from the gospel. It is essentially about turning exegesis into praxis. Graham Tomlin, in his brilliant book on evangelism *The Provocative Church*, comments that the New Testament rarely contains appeals to Christians to get out and *tell* their friends about Jesus. This is not because the writers were not concerned that people came to faith in Christ, but rather because they did not believe that this was the way to do it. Rather, he says, it is about a way of living that displays something special and distinctive and intrigues others to discover more. Genuine evangelism, he says, invites people to the transformed life because 'things could and should be better than they are and because our present way of life is not the only way of life. And because we have heard news that there is another king, another kingdom, under whose rule things are very different.'[7] In order to participate in this we need to undertake experiences that will change us, shape us and help us to grow. This spiritual stretching can be as simple as a person giving the life of faith a chance – actually a common and highly contemporary theme for many looking to live life at a different level. Tomlin tells a story of a young student who had carefully weighed up the pros and cons of becoming a Christian but was at a loss which way to turn. The answer was to 'try it' for a few weeks, to step out of the spiritual no man's land of procrastination and actually live for a while believing it was true, living faith out in practical ways. Tomlin says:

> He came back a week later. I could tell immediately that some-thing was different. The worried frown had transformed into a definite smile. 'I did what you said, and it worked! I started to live as if it was true; now I know it is true.' He had begun to experience transformation.[8]

Being a person of faith should mean that we are always seek-ing to develop our spiritual awareness. It means us living in the knowledge that we just might have the capacity to live by the energy and compulsion of an *inner* life rather than skim-ming on the surface of what is rational and material. One way to stretch our experience of God is to travel inwards and practise prayer in such a way that it genuinely transforms the person we have become, with all our ingrained habits and selfish immovability. But this can be scary because as well as coming face to face with the living God who moves us onwards, first we have to confront the tangled and harried parts of our-selves. Ignatian biblical meditation is a well-documented method of prayer and one that is becoming increasingly popular as people thirst for ways of understanding the presence of God within as well as the God 'out there'. It is in this holy inner domain that God speaks, in startling and surprising ways, often knocking out of us the idea we subconsciously retain of a God made in our own image who suits our personal spiritual needs.

At theological college it was part of student training to under-take a five-week 'Retreat in Daily Life', when we learnt to pray using the Ignatian technique. I took part in this spiritual adventure twice during my three years of training; the first time my life was rosy, the second time life was painful and crisis-laden. Such is the potential power of this method of praying that a spiritual companion is needed to help discernment, particularly for those who might struggle to understand what comes from God and what does not. This was my question on one occasion, deep into an imaginative meditation on the turning of the tables in the Temple, when Jesus kicked over the tables with what felt like a disturbing amount of violence and anger. That experience, at the time, felt distressing. I had been used to the idea of a God who had the capacity for anger intellectually but felt uncomfortable about experiencing this with immediacy on a personal level. It took some further work before I realized that my frustration at not being allowed to express anger as a child was wrapped up in this, and that my anger had been unhelpfully buried. My guide helped me not only to recognize this but to move on (a stretching experience in itself), as well as to begin to explore that an 'angry Christ' is an acceptable image of Jesus. *The Angry Christ* by the artist Lino Pontebon is one that continues to stretch people's idea of the meek and mild Jesus.[9] Emerging from the historical reality of the Marcos regime in the Philippines, the artist highlights the plight of indigenous peoples at the hands of unscrupulous developers, as well as the exploitation brought by the international sex trade. It is an image that continues potentially to catalyse us out of the complacency of our familiar faith contexts.

The point about this stretching, if it is genuinely holy, is that we do not do it alone. The Incarnation means that we cannot dislocate our lives from the capacious life of God that flows through the arteries of humanity. If we are new at the gym we might have a personal trainer who shows us how to use the machines so that they stretch our muscles but do not do us irreparable harm. It is the same with the spiritual journey. A woman who comes to see me for spiritual companionship described a dream she had of wandering around in the garden where there was a large dark tomb, similar to Mary Magdalene on the first Easter morning. Like most of us, she has unresolved issues in her life that she is more than aware of. In her dream there appeared a gloomy and slightly sinister opening to a dark cave. Unable to venture inside, she worried that she could not seem to take the next step and spent the time procrastinating, feeling an ambivalent sense of intrigue as to what was inside as well as a deep fear to step forward. I sensed her yearning to go in, and suggested to her that she return to the scene, and imagine sitting outside the cave. The next stage would be to imagine herself in Christ's presence and to see whether, going with him, she might be able to walk into the darkness. This kind of stretching is, ironically, often about *staying* in a 'place', within which we recognize an unresolved, thorny issue that might make us feel uneasy or awkward for a time; however, when we stretch and face it the rewards have far-reaching effects. The desert fathers and mothers had a saying: 'Go, sit in your cell, and your cell will teach you everything.'

One way in which the soul stretch and the physical stretch work together is the idea of the pilgrimage, a word that derives from the Latin *peregrinatus*, meaning a person who travelled literally 'across fields' or over a long distance. The word has come to be understood as a journey for which God remains the focus and reason, or alternatively a journey that has some deep motivation and purpose, where the pilgrim expects to be challenged and changed. The traveller is opened up not only to the meteorological elements but to the process of what might be described as 'soul-mining'. In earlier centuries, pilgrimage could be a hard and dangerous practice, with travellers being stretched to their physical limits – hungry, cold and ill, attacked and robbed. In the early Middle Ages, spreading the gospel became the main aim of pilgrimage, while in Celtic Christianity leaving the security of your home for the sake of Christ, even if it meant martyrdom on the way, was highly regarded. David Osborne cites the Australian novelist Bruce Chatwin, who wrote about the wanderings of Aboriginal people in his famous book

The Songlines, suggesting that travelling is in fact a primeval urge among many human beings, and that it is the accepted settled life that is the abnormality in many societies around the globe. If this is so, Osborne says, then maybe the Church needs to encourage people to stretch faith through the context of travel rather than remaining somewhere that feels safe: 'In the Bible the two images of the journey and the place of rest are in tension with one another. The journey leads to the Promised Land but the hope of the Promised Land draws the traveller on.'[10] In a similar way, Jesus moved from place to place, and sometimes on his journey he himself was surprised and challenged. A Syro-Phoenician woman made him reconsider his own mission, while his own town of Nazareth became so incensed by his words and actions that they rejected him and threatened death. Every genuine pilgrimage should retain a sense of openness, and it is this openness – this sense of not knowing what will happen on the journey – that becomes the stretching dynamic.

One of my favourite films is *The Way*. It is the story of Thomas Avery, an American ophthalmologist, who hears that his son Daniel has died tragically in the Pyrenees while making the famous pilgrimage along the Camino de Santiago. Thomas journeys to Spain and decides to walk the pilgrimage route himself, scattering the ashes of his son at strategic points along the road. Engrossed in his own inevitable grief, Thomas is initially antisocial, but his solo journey collides with that of three strangers walking the road. All are walking the *camino* for personal reasons, which come to light as friendships are established. Along the way, Thomas sees visions of his son, meeting folk, laughing and experiencing life in all its joyfulness, which stretch his muddied and engrained opinion of his son, as he realizes that he had perhaps not appreciated Daniel's life-embracing attitude. Although none of the characters is walking the route for specifically religious reasons, the life of God feels deeply embedded in the story. They are all searching for a deeper meaning in life and perhaps seeking healing from unhappy or traumatic past experiences – the loss of a child, an unhappy marriage and the frustration of non-creativity. In essence, *The Way* is a film about being stretched – through the experience of grief, through walking long distances and through the learning of tolerance that is inevitably involved in the love and acceptance of others in all their irritations and imperfections. In the end, a sense emerges that, through the challenge, the characters, each with their own broken parts, are somehow transformed, healed a little, and given hope for the next part of their lives.

There is within us the capacity to be aware of what I would describe as 'the divine nudge' – the gentle but persistent pull or push of a God who wants us to be taken and filled by the Spirit. This nudge asks us to be ever vigilant, on the look-out to say and do things that stretch us, taking us out of our comfort zones, wherever these might be, believing that we can never do enough for the mission and justice of God. There is always more that be done to help the Christian life to be visibly distinctive for the sake of implementing the alternative vision God has for the world – the kingdom of God. The Spirit is gentle but it is also compelling and conscience-awakening. Brian McLaren, in his book *We Make the Road by Walking*, talks about the simple image of walking – the desire for movement that propels children to get up onto their feet and walk bravely on into life. The image of walking is everywhere in the Scriptures, he says. We are told to walk in the Spirit, to walk in the light, to walk in love and in faith. To be a disciple and someone who lives a prayerful life is to walk in the footsteps of the one we adore and want to follow, even if he leads us through tangled places and into a hard land. McLaren writes:

> When we desire to be filled with the Spirit, the Spirit begins to transform our desires so that God's desires become our own. Instead of doing the right thing because we *have* to, we do the right thing because we *want* to – because we are learning to truly desire goodness. Once our desires are being changed, a revolution is set in motion.[11]

Stretch in practice

Individual

- Reflect on where your own 'comfort zones' are – physically, emotionally and spiritually. Do you need to move beyond them? Is God asking you to undertake something you might find challenging for his sake? Perhaps this is the right time?
- Is there a way of deepening your knowledge of yourself and God through learning a new way of praying or reading books that might prove a contrast to the ones you normally choose?
- Can you say 'yes' to a new role or responsibility for your church or community that might stretch you and your understanding of how God interacts in the world?
- Think back to a time in your life when you were really stretched through the voluntary undertaking of a task or project. What did you learn through the experience?

Corporate

- Reflect on the current 'stretching' your church encourages.
- Is there a future project or ministry that could become a sign of God's kingdom in your own community and context that would stretch your church?
- How can you stretch people's understanding and knowledge of God through teaching and worship? How can horizons be expanded gently?
- Think about ways in which you as a leader can gently encourage people to step out of a place of fear to challenge themselves for God (for example, being part of a Christian Aid street collection).

6

Thank
An attitude of gratitude

———•◆•———

Wear gratitude like a cloak and it will feed every corner of your life. (Rumi)

As both a feeling and an awareness, gratitude is a virtue with ethical consequences. When we feel most grateful, it is impossible to be cruel or callous, brutal or indifferent. (Marcus Borg)[1]

'I don't have everything I love but I love everything I have.' This is Rosie's mantra. Rosie Pinto De Carvalho lives with her husband Marcos and seven children on the edge of a landfill site in one of Rio de Janeiro's favelas. The members of her family spend their lives collecting plastic bottles and other items to be sold for recycling. The house she lives in leaks but she is gradually saving enough money to build another dwelling. Rosie and her story featured in the third programme in BBC 2's *Welcome to Rio* series, which looked at the vibrant and paradoxical life in the favelas of this city of overwhelming vivacity before the onset of the World Cup in Brazil in June 2014. Like many people living in quite a lot of poverty, Rosie's life is complicated and often frustrating. Clearly the matriarch at the heart of her brood, energizing the others and making the financial cogs turn, she still had to rely on her husband Marcos to negotiate the verbal business of buying and selling – everything from trash to the pigs the family occasionally sell. But as the rain begins to fall, soaking the inside of the house where children are sleeping, Rosie speaks these words: 'I don't have everything I love but I love everything I have.'

It can be easy for us who do not live in such conditions to romanticize poverty, or make ourselves feel better by saying, 'It's not as bad as all that; these people are happy, after all,' but the triumph of this series was the clear message that life in Rio's shanty towns, although far from ideal, has a bright and burning energy that many relish. Such energy establishes a genuine level of happiness that enriches the people who live there and spills over into the rest of the city. Edward Watts, the director of the series, took the approach that it was an '(ad) venture into rough, crooked places to discover what lies beyond clichéd stories'. The message to the viewers was, 'Yeah, what we have might not be much but we have the important things in life – family, friends, people to help, joy and always the opportunity for a party.'

What is clear is that gratitude as an attitude to life often comes more easily the less we have materially. Rosie wanted her house built – a natural yearning especially when you have seven children to feed – but in the messy and far-from-ideal interim her joyfulness and gratitude for the life she lived was as clear as a crystal sea. It's my belief that when we live with a continuous and fairly stable quality of life it is more challenging to have feelings of gratitude as hard strata running as a constant through our lives, where medical care and celebrating Christmas bountifully are givens. We get used to the ease and comfort we have, of stocked fridges and solid roofs. The fact that our children go to school every day and that most of us have a car on the drive, friends, and water coming from a tap creates the background wallpaper of daily unacknowledgement. Of course we are grateful, we cry, but it's hard to *feel* it when our lives are safe and stable and we have plenty to live on that is easily available, fresh and reliable. It is when things are removed from us or we choose to live without something important that the opportunity is created for gratitude to be more keenly felt. And when whatever it is that is absent is returned or resumed, it rushes back, knocking us over like a surfer's wave. This is perhaps particularly true with our health. Rhidian Brook, during his travels in Africa, describes a meal he shared with AIDS sufferers.

> The woman called us back to eat and I was asked to say grace. I started with a thanks for the food but soon moved on to thanks for Patrick, and then on to his mother, his brother and sisters and the volunteers from Compassion and then the community. It was a proper African grace, missing no opportunity or object to be grateful for and ending – mindful of absent fathers – with thanks to the Father of all. Why does saying grace come easier in places where there is materially less to thank God for?[2]

Thanking God is at the heart of our faith and worship. The word 'eucharist' means thanksgiving. We thank God for his gifts, and primarily the gift of Jesus Christ, whose memory and living presence is embodied on Sundays, played out in the ultimate ritualistic meal of Communion. Gratitude has the potential to colour how we live – an echo of grace. It has the potential to turn around the most stubborn of cynicisms and bleak approaches to life, for what it attempts to do is say to us, 'Be grateful for what you have – not tomorrow or next year but right now.' Gratitude has the power to rinse our consciousness through with a refreshed attitude of appreciation. But like most concepts of spirituality this needs conscious and regular effort, which sounds like work but can result in genuine inner freedom if we practise and build upon it.

In our culture we have, for the most part, stopped being grateful and have become instead expectant, often insistently so. We have also become more impatient and perhaps intolerant than we used to be. Both of these are enemies of gratitude. But for us as followers of Christ, fostering an 'attitude of gratitude' becomes, like all the concepts in this book, potentially transformative; it has the energy to transform the approach we take to how we live our lives. It transforms our attitude to how we eat, what we own and what and how we give, both financially and of our time through human loving effort. Gratitude does its best to walk all over guilt as well. Living in gratefulness means that we do things because we are thankful, not because we feel we should. Materially it should help the ceasing of oppressive comparison with what others have and achieve as well.

The story of the ten lepers remains one of the archetypal passages on gratitude in the Bible (Luke 17.11–19). The fact that the leper who returns to Jesus was from the underclass of the Samaritans, reviled and unpopular, is of consequence in the light of the above illustration of who is likely to be the most grateful for what they have in our world. This man would not just have been healed of the physical discomforts of his painful disease, he would have been enabled to return, presumably to his home, where he might have had family and friends. Because of the social restraints of the disease, he would up to now have been forced to be a wandering spirit – doubly vilified, both abandoned by his own kin and despised by other Jews who were lepers too. So perhaps his potential double gratitude made him search out Jesus for a second time. Jesus was, I'm sure, pleased that the man had returned to thank him but his brusque response says more about the ungrateful nine than about the Samaritan. Yet the nine lepers had obeyed Jesus in good faith – they were on their way to see the priest, which was the correct and obedient requirement within Jewish law for people who had recovered from a disease that made them unclean. But they were nevertheless lacking something inherent to the spirit of the gospel, namely grace. Alyce McKenzie illuminates the subtle difference in the words Jesus uses to describe the healing of the nine Jewish lepers. The word *tharizo* means 'to be made clean and healed of a disease', which is different from the word that Jesus uses for the one Samaritan leper who returns. Here he uses *sozo*, or 'to be healed of spiritual disease and death'. In other words, Luke makes the theological point that only the foreigner is grateful for the grace received. The ungrateful nine exemplify the blinded attitude of the Jewish people towards Jesus' mission, whereas the Samaritan is prophetic of the future inclusive response of non-Jews to and for the gospel.[3]

This story is not meant to promote a slavish discipline of remembering to thank others, like a child painfully writing thank you letters to distant relatives after Christmas. It is rather a thought-provoking passage that helps us reflect on why gratitude is so vital for our spiritual well-being and why it is deeply connected with love, as suggested at the beginning of the chapter. Gratitude, for people of faith, is about the connection of what is given as gift with the ultimate giver behind the gift. A developed grateful attitude keeps us focused on the God who gives life every day; maybe this, as Alyce McKenzie suggests, is why Jesus laments those who do not return. It is the lament of a loss of connection with a divine power that gives all as gift.

Living gratefully is one of the simplest and most ancient forms of prayer. St Ignatius of Loyola felt strongly that gratitude should be the basic response to God's abiding love. He wrote that ingratitude 'is the most abominable of sins, and is to be detested in the sight of the Creator and Lord by all of God's creatures for it is the forgetting of the graces, benefits and blessings received'.[4] Ignatian spirituality understands gratitude as more than a transient feeling and rather as an abiding vision that always recognizes the gift-nature of everything. The final section of the Spiritual Exercises (the Contemplation to Attain Love) devised by Ignatius holds gratitude at its heart. First is the belief that everything is gift, from creation to redemption, as well as the individual good things each person 'receives', and there is encouragement to spend time contemplating these things. Second is the belief that attempting to deepen our sense of gratitude encourages us to become 'practitioners of love for God', expanding our sense of God's generosity to us. Spilling over from this is the idea that God's presence dwells in all created things, and is never inert but rather dynamic and active in our lives. God continually invites us to grow in gratitude by becoming more and more mindful of his presence and activity.[5]

Maybe within this is what Dietrich Bonhoeffer says in *Life Together* – that we prevent God from giving us great spiritual gifts because we do not give thanks for our daily gifts enough.

> We pray for the big things and forget to give thanks for the ordinary, small (and yet really not small) gifts. How can God entrust great things to someone who will not thankfully receive from him the little things? If we do not give thanks daily for the Christian fellowship in which we have been placed, even where there is no great experience, no discoverable riches, but much weakness, small faith and difficulty; if on the contrary we only keep complaining to God that everything is so paltry and petty, so far from what we expected, then we hinder God from letting our fellowship grow according to the measure and riches which are there for us all in Jesus Christ.[6]

This is the lot of the nine lepers; living as we do with a high quality of life in the West, we need to make sure that it is not ours as well.

When we live in a grateful domestic and ecclesial environment it makes a difference. More than anything, developing an ongoing and growing spirit of gratitude in the places we live and work means that it is harder for us to take others for granted, to assume they will always be there, undertaking certain jobs and roles. We all know how it feels when we put gargantuan effort into a particular task or project and then no one takes any notice, or thanks us. After a particularly difficult year (and after a previous bad experience at an annual parochial church meeting) I phoned up our two churchwardens. Having sat through this meeting, when the world and his wife were thanked for their contributions over the year, I was shocked and angry that no one, not even the wardens, had got up to thank my husband, the rector. Uncomfortably aware that such behaviour could be viewed as deeply unchristian I hoped they would view my reaction as that of a concerned wife. Since that time he has always been thanked – not effusively but certainly sincerely – and I have been grateful. If our contributions are never acknowledged, it is only human that we react by not putting quite so much effort and love into what we do. Or maybe I'm just not very saintly.

When we are in leadership we need to thank others, not only for what they do but for who they are. Such thanking should become a regular part of ministry, public and private, even though the demon of forgetting someone is always lurking around the corner. In *Secrets of Resilient People* John Lees states that one of the reasons that gratitude is so important is because it reflects a healthy (and for us holy) understanding that good things come from outside of ourselves. This is what so many of the Psalms point to – an uncontainable joyful awareness of the goodness and greatness of God the Creator. Psalm 138 begins a set of effusive verses by thanking God:

> I give you thanks, O LORD, with my whole heart;
> Before the gods I sing your praise;
> I bow down toward your holy temple
> And give thanks to your name for your steadfast
>   love and your faithfulness.

Here gratitude is not just a muttered aside but a heartfelt, exuberant, whole-person sentiment – *with my whole heart*. Gratitude eclipses all the other 'gods' that creep into place, establishing them in our life's priorities and inspiring worship. But Lees, himself a professional career strategist and Anglican priest, says that we need also to be mindful about how we express our thankfulness. If we say thank you too much there is the danger of appearing insincere, or as though we are simply trying to please others. Living gratefully means learning to express our thanks genuinely, like the Psalmist but choosing to express this carefully – perhaps with occasional careful gifts as well as words.

In our contemporary context this belief can be seen being worked out creatively in community projects such as the Gratitude Graffiti Project in Maplewood, New Jersey. This is a simple, 40-day practice of 'purposeful appreciation of one's life through interactive art'. The project asks residents to identify a source of gratitude in their lives and to provide an outlet to express this creatively. Gratitude 'stops' are created so that people walking by are grabbed by the visual effect of what hundreds of local people have written about what is good in their lives and why they are thankful for them. Created by Lucila McElroy and Candice Davenport, Gratitude Graffiti has inspired other communities around the world to live always within the expanding parameters of gratitude. A local business who participated in this stated: 'This was a heartfelt statement of gratitude expression, and the timing could not have been better. After the storm [Hurricane Sandy], our clients, young and old alike, still had an abundance of gratitude to report . . . the response was overwhelmingly positive.'[7]

Gratitude reshapes us, emotionally and spiritually, so that we become redirected towards God once again, whether we can name this or not. Gratitude is deeply subversive because it turns on its head many of the values that insidiously squeeze themselves into most parts of modern life. Living life gratefully has the potential to inspire others to interpret their own lives from a different perspective.

Our subconscious attitude to gratitude, though, is more often than not understood as some kind of completion. Think of a gift. We receive that gift and we say 'thank you' in some way. Hopefully, we continue to enjoy the gift and it occasionally reminds us of the giver, but after the initial expression of gratitude that tends to be the end of the process or event. David Steindl-Rast, a Benedictine monk and teacher, has reflected over a number of decades on the issue of gratitude. One significant implication of living a life of deep thankfulness, he says, is that it can be the beginning of a new or renewed relationship with others and the world. He has written 'A Pledge for Grateful Living', which speaks about five human struggles that can be overcome to reorient a life.[8] Entitlement is transformed into gratitude itself, greed turns into generosity, apathy into creativity, violence into non-violence and fear into courage.

So the concept of 'thank' is not passive but highly active and even potentially subversive. Thank refuses to be put into the position of victim, thank turns on its head 'bad luck' and takes control of a situation by voluntarily promoting a positive outlook.

But the most important element of thank is always the connection with something beyond ourselves. Steindl-Rast says this: 'We cannot essentially be grateful to things or an impersonal power like "life" or nature.' He identifies a threefold dynamic of heartfelt gratitude: first, something that is offered to and for us, second, the recognition that this is given to us freely, and third, the return of our heartfelt thanks for the gift, which, if it is genuine and unadulterated, brings a sense of deep joy. He makes the point that this threefold expression is a dynamic that connects many of the world's religions, explicit in tangible rituals and verbal prayers. The Anglican baptism service, for example, thanks God for 'the gift of these children entrusted to our care . . . So that through our love they may know your love' – an acknowledgement that a gift has been granted through the pairing of two human people, but with a recognition wrapped within this of the mystery of procreation, thus linking with the ultimate Creator.

In an essay, 'A Vision for the World', Steindl-Rast makes the distinction between gratefulness and giving thanks. Gratefulness happens before thinking, he believes, in that brief gap between realization and thought:

> It is the spontaneous response of the human heart to that which is gratuitously given. This gratefulness releases energy. In the gap of surprise before the first thought comes, the powerful surge of an intelligence that far surpasses thought takes hold of us.

Here is a simple but concrete example. One June Sunday last year, I came home from taking the morning's services and sat down in our sunny garden with a cup of coffee. This was no mere pause in my day; it was contemplated with the delicious notion that for three months I had some time to rest, read and study, because that day was the beginning of my sabbatical from current ministry. But it was not to be. Twenty minutes into that time soaking up the sun I became aware of someone stampeding through the front door anxiously calling my name. My husband, having rapidly experienced a dark shadow in his eye, had sensibly gone to the optician. A detached retina was diagnosed. That afternoon we were at the hospital and early the next day we were at another – he on the operating table undergoing laser eye treatment. The result – a missed holiday and my much anticipated time out from ministry evaporating for a few weeks of further work. But the gratitude that rushed headlong after this ordeal was heartfelt as it dawned on us both that he could easily have lost his sight in that eye. Gratitude – for the vigilance of the optician, for the NHS, for the fact that I could actually step into his shoes easily, and for a loving and supportive church community who also rallied round. During that three weeks I was inundated with meals, cakes, offers of help from all directions, so that any lingering resentment on my part swiftly disappeared.

Thanking is the 'thinking work' that is done when gratitude has so transformed us that we are inspired to change the way we act. In other words, it is an opportunity to break out of whatever destructive or unproductive behaviour we find ourselves rutted into. For 'when you are grateful, your heart is open – open towards others, open for surprise'.[9] More than anything, gratefulness dispels our sometimes pernicious sense of alienation because it reminds us that our lives are deeply entwined with those of others, that we would fail to function without the contributions of many people – those we know and those we are completely unaware of. When gratefulness overtakes us we place ourselves within this 'network of belonging' and we also say 'yes' to the spreading out and joyful power of love. Thomas Merton writes:

> If we are not grateful to God, we cannot taste the joy of finding Him in His creation. To be ungrateful is to admit that we do not know Him, and that we love His creatures not for His sake but for our own. Unless we are grateful for our own existence, we do not know who we are, and we have not yet discovered what it really means to be and to live. No matter how high an estimate we may have of our own goodness, that estimate is too low unless we realise that all we have comes to us from God.[10]

Thank in practice

Individual

- Use the Ignatian way of prayer called examen, where the day is reviewed by discerning where God's activity has been tangibly felt. This exercise can be a powerful one in terms of identifying the 'good things' in the day even when that day hasn't felt very positive. Identify five or ten 'good things' for which you can genuinely offer thanks. If you want to go further, identify things that are problematic for you and try just 'turning them around'. An honest example from my own life was feeling growing resentment at the number of my children's friends I seem to be perpetually feeding and having around the house. But 'turned around', my frustration (and maybe anxiety over cost and a lack of privacy in my own space) became gratitude that our home is a lively and happy place where young people (often who come from broken homes) can feel at ease, and huge gratitude that my children are popular and have genuine friends. This exercise, when practised regularly, can alter how we look at our lives generally.
- If you have children, begin a 'thank you' jar. At a meal or particular time of day everyone thinks of something or someone

they want to say thank you for. When the jar is filled, pick out one thing for each member of your family and decide to do or buy something associated with that thing or person.

- Identify ten things you want to say thank you for each day. But don't just name them, dwell on them as well.

Corporate

- Most churches are at least moderately good at saying thank you to people, particularly when they stop doing a particular job or ministry or when they leave. Important as this is, if you are in leadership think about those who often remain unthanked, perhaps because their contribution goes un-recognized or because their role is not a high-profile job, or simply because that person has *always* done something. It can mean a tremendous amount if we can think of ways of expressing our gratitude to such people, not necessarily publicly but in small, behind-the-scenes ways. There needs to be an awareness of those who tend to fall through the net who might be hurt or offended because they have been missed out.

- Constructing services around the idea of gratitude can help people focus on the goodness and greatness of God as well as encouraging everyone to understand life as primarily gift rather than something to be coped with or that we have constant high expectations of. Find good biblical passages where gratitude is genuinely expressed and root this by providing rituals within a service for people to express gratitude tangibly; this can be moving and contemplative at the same time.

- Write a contemporary 'liturgy of thanksgiving' and put together a sequence of visual images to run alongside this.

- Harvest is traditionally a time when congregations are encouraged to thank God for his ongoing creative power through the natural world.

7

Deep
Where have all the wise people gone?

———•◦•———

> Wisdom is not a product bought over the counter or available instantly and effortlessly at the touch of a button. It takes time, draws on the past, embraces the shared understandings of the community, and in humility concedes its limitations set against the inscrutable reality of God.
>
> (Rod Garner, *How To Be Wise*)[1]

> Look inside yourself. You are more than what you have become.
>
> (Mufasa's Ghost, *The Lion King*)

During my curacy, in an environment I sometimes found bleak, I headed out one day with a friend into the greenness of Derbyshire. This county is littered with the leftovers of mining heritage, now tourist attractions, and we came across the entrance to the Blue John Mine. Without a thought we donned hard hats and sat in tiny trains that winched us deep into the bowels of the earth. After the trains came small boats and ever-decreasing physical space. At this point on our trip my body started to behave in an unnatural and frightening way. I began to sweat, my heart pounded and I realized that I was hyperventilating. If it had not been for the measured and calm talking of my companion I dread to think what would have happened. I held it together by concentrating my mind on the idea of rational safety until we arrived at a larger cave, which provided me with the physical and psychological space to feel better. But all was not completely well until we returned above ground and the fresh air. I had not previously been aware that I am highly claustrophobic in deep places, and I have never ventured into such a confined space since that day.

It is potentially frightening to go deep into the earth. It is a similarly frightening prospect to delve deep within ourselves, to try to understand better the people that we are. And it can be disquieting to begin to feel how God might be found in the layers of how we are made – so much so that many do not even 'go there' and prefer to leave the idea of 'inner life' well alone. We live in an age where expanding our life experience existentially has become the new god. Over one weekend, my son (although admittedly it was his birthday and the end of term) enjoyed a trip to Alton Towers, went paintballing, and participated in the tree-top adventure course – 'Go Ape'. Such experiences entertain and occupy us; they stretch our experience of being human at one level by increasing our achievements and entertainment. But it is only when we reflect and dwell on our experiences that they begin to form and change us. The things that our contemporary culture holds dear – the accumulation of knowledge and skill, choice, travel and entertainment – are useless to people of faith unless they are applied to our life as well as connected with the life of God. Rod Garner, in his book *How To Be Wise*, puts it succinctly:

> The good life that has at its heart the aim of a practical wisdom that shapes our moral identity retains its appeal, particularly when so much of the moral landscape seems fuzzy and the white noise of the information age invites us to know everything, except what is worth knowing.[2]

But one day we will perhaps run out of such 'experiences' and there will be no more undiscovered places to explore. The phrase 'been there, done that' says it all.

But our fragmented world needs individuals of depth and wisdom, people who have reflected on their life experiences to an extent that they are able to offer something uniquely life-giving to others who seek it. Yet every age generates problematic situations specific to its time, and people of faith today have the huge resource of being able to look back into history and see those who have walked before us, to look to people who have, in the words of Sam Wells, 'asked questions as big as ours, and found truth as deep as we have'. Wells goes on:

> Their wisdom is the template for ours. That's what the scriptures are for Christians – the wisdom of those who have encountered God. Our willingness to read scripture and to be read by scripture is a sign of our humility that we take our place as small players in a huge story, the general shape of which can't be determined or ruined by us.[3]

Wisdom is not difficult to recognize. Sometimes we are aware that we are sitting in its presence or inadvertently benefiting from its judgements. The environment that the early evangelists were working in understood the idea of wisdom very clearly because wisdom was then a sought-after characteristic. In his communications to the Christian communities in Greece, Paul says that this wisdom has reached its fulfilment in the person of Jesus. He draws this out by teaching that it is only when we internalize the teachings, but more crucially the actual person, of Jesus and are transformed by this experience that we acquire wisdom. Another way of describing this is attaining 'the mind of Christ'.

Christian people, and perhaps clergy in particular, are in a unique position to live some of this mystery, because faith requires them to reflect and focus on God every time prayer happens, every time a sermon is listened to, each time a theological book is studied, and each time we reflect on our beauty as well as our fallen-ness. Many people still approach those who are ordained with the sense that clergy hold the key to some kind of mystic, esoteric knowledge that will help people whose lives feel blocked or meaningless to move forwards. Most of us need advice and careful consideration from others at many stages in our lives, whether or not we are people of faith, and we feel instinctively that there might be a right person to offer it and are able to we seek them out. It is the perception, perhaps, that some people are living their lives at a depth that is distinctively different from a material one. These people have worked hard at understanding what it means to feel and be alive at a deeper level than most, with all that this potentially involves. Their inner spirit may communicate a peace and knowledge that can be tangibly felt. Philip Newell likens such people to the Indian tradition of the *sanyassi*, where men in their golden years abandon all outward claims to possessions and family status and simply wander as people of prayer. In the East such men are marked not by what they do, say or teach but merely by their spirit. He says, 'Similarly people will gather round a guru simply to *be in his presence*, and, in a sense to catch peace from him at a level profounder than words.'[4]

Unlike many of the prayerful concepts thus far, wisdom cannot be 'achieved', for it proves notoriously slippery. If we consider ourselves wise then we are probably a long way from being so, for there is no place within wisdom for an inflated or arrogant sense of who we are and what we might be able to offer others. Wisdom is something that happens slowly, over time, like the gradual growth of the rings of a tree. As with adoration, wisdom is something that we like the sound of but to contemporary ways of living and being it seems archaic and out of fashion – both in church and in society. 'Deep' explores the idea of how we might walk deliberately into wisdom in three distinctive ways: by returning and ruminating on the everyday experiences that we live with, by learning how to step back from our capabilities and achievements by allowing others to flourish and contribute, and by a refreshed acceptance that God is also the opposite of this – 'other and mystery'. These factors of 'deep' are all facets of wisdom and are about enabling others to be affirmed in faith and ministry.

The Greek philosopher Socrates asked every new student, 'Are you in love with wisdom?' This is what philosophy means; the word is made up of two Greek words, *phileo* (I love) and *sophia* (wisdom). The Jewish wisdom tradition incorporated the idea that wisdom always stemmed from the nature and purpose of God, as well as being connected to the experience of everyday life and its challenges. As Christopher Cocksworth says, 'Essentially the Jewish wisdom tradition seeks to answer two great questions: "Who is God?" and "How does God want us to live?"'[5] The book of Proverbs, for example, contains wise advice on how to live, while Ecclesiastes suggests that life will be ultimately empty unless we understand our need for God and his purpose for us. Proverbs 3.19 reminds us that wisdom can be found in the very stuff of life; Proverbs 8.4 says that God makes this wisdom potentially available to all people: 'To you, O people, I call, and my cry is to all that live.' Wisdom is bound up with life and life is gift.

The Wisdom tradition tells us that if we ruminate and reflect on often quite prosaic and ordinary experiences we just might gain wisdom. In 1 Kings 3.3–38 Solomon, aware of his need for God to help him in the early years of his reign, prays for the gift of wisdom over and above everything else. With immense issues to deal with, like the rule of a sprawling kingdom, the reconstruction of the Temple and keeping warring nations in abeyance, God's wisdom enables Solomon to deal with a very domestic situation. Two poor women vie for his attention, asking him to make a heart-breaking decision. Both mothers, one of their children has died and both are claiming to be the parent of the one who is alive. Solomon calls the women's bluff by threatening to cut the remaining child in half, and the real mother is discovered. Here wisdom is needed in the very stuff of everyday life – joy and sorrow. And the manner of the situation is such that it requires the wisdom not only of Solomon but of God.

Wisdom for ancient Israel was complex, questioning and sometimes paradoxical. It was concerned with moral values but had the capacity (as in the above story) to expose human selfishness and foolishness. But it was also, as Rod Garner makes clear, about the ordinary things of life – health and hospitality, about the proper use of resources and the obligation we have towards one another. We continue this tradition, as wisdom is built by ruminating and returning to those life events that are significant to us, where we perceive God's presence to have been most in evidence, in the past as well as in the present. This is summed up in the words of Ephesians 1.17–19; Paul prays that Christ will give to the people 'a spirit of wisdom and revelation . . . so that, with *the eyes of your hearts enlightened*, you may know what is the hope to which [God] has called you, what are the riches of his glorious inheritance among the saints, and what is the immeasurable greatness of his power for us who believe'. We may not be called to make momentous decisions on matters of government, but perhaps our children, friends or parishioners may come to us, in crisis or indecision, needing wise and loving words from us that hopefully have faith as their bedrock. In my experience as priest, what people seek from those they perceive to be wise are words that arise from lived-out and prayed-through experience. Essentially they want something that they can relate to. Wisdom is a returning back to, rather than a running away from, our beautiful yet murky humanity, woven together with the profundities of the holy. It is when we chew over those very ordinary experiences that wisdom is born, together with the recognition that we need something more from God – that within our life, we realize, like the author of Ecclesiastes, that 'something is missing and its absence hurts'.[6]

Wise people often display a natural or developed attitude of reverent awe before the holiness and otherness of God. The story of Ruth, although not a traditional story of biblical wisdom, is one where several wise choices are made with unconscious nobility and genuine humility within the ups and downs of everyday life.

The lives of Ruth and Naomi have become problematic – both their husbands have died, leaving them physically bereft of family and support. Ruth, with determined zeal, chooses to stay with her mother-in-law Naomi. This idea of wise choices continues with the act of harvesting and gathering the excess crops – the women use what is already available to them, then and there. For us, wisdom can often be found in the experiences that prove familiar to us, those that are close at hand if only we can develop a contemplative way of reflecting on them and their further significance. The story continues: after making connections with Boaz, Boaz gives to Ruth more food to take way – in Ruth 3.15 he gives her six extra measures of barley to take back to her mother-in-law. We ourselves get much, then, from delving deep, using and reflecting on the experiences from our past and present, to think about where the action and presence of God is manifest.

In Proverbs 8 wisdom is personified as a woman; like Ruth, she urges upon others right action, the love of truth and the importance of right instruction that proves more precious than jewels. The very essence of wisdom is associated with those qualities exemplified in the character of Ruth – an openness to God's will leading into the future with loyalty and humility, and knowing what is important for a fruitful life. For Ruth and Naomi this was the establishing of stable foundations for their future in securing a second husband for Ruth, not through manipulation but by a genuine willingness to allow God's goodness to unfold. And Boaz sought the opinions of those who had a greater right to take Ruth as wife – wisdom is seen in asking the views of others as well as in following a proper and honourable procedure. Wisdom is both immanent (among and with us) and transcendent (available as a power that is beyond us).

Wisdom is often associated with old age, and this can be lived out by a rightful 'stepping back' or 'letting go' of the busyness and urgency of life. But whether we are in the prime of our life or ministry or in our latter years, we can still take much from reflecting on this idea. In my own congregation, Don, a previous churchwarden and retired professional man, displays a depth of wisdom and spirituality. Never garrulous, when he speaks people listen to his careful words. Don also has the ability to know that at his stage in life he has to step back from being in the forefront of the cut and thrust of energetic ministry and mission, but he contains an emotional security about this. For people like him there is the sense of allowing others, often younger, to take risks, 'to have their day as well as their say', demonstrating their own gifts even if this results in an almighty mess. One of his gifts is understanding how to use his past expertise to take up tasks that inevitably save the clergy extra work, or ones they find tedious. Another element he brings is the ability to organize and participate in the prayer ministry that underpins the whole parish behind the scenes. Don is someone I would approach for advice; I like him enormously because his personal wisdom contains a vital sense of perspective, humour and is never patronizing. For many it feels hallowed and cathartic and stable to be near his loving presence.

Perhaps the archetypal wise folk in the New Testament are Simeon and Anna, who wait patiently for the sight of the infant Jesus. Inhabiting the shadows of the Temple, they nevertheless do not lose the sense of the big picture of the significance of who Jesus was to be. Their perspective was deeper and broader than the traditional expectation that assumed the Messiah would come clad in power and military glory. Spiritual writers through the centuries, such as John Donne, have written about the deep knowledge that we are really not very important in relation to the grand scheme of things. Wisdom is about the recognition that our human lifespan is encased, part of a much greater, more timeless eternity. As priests and theologians, we are called in our role to 'commune with the divine and bring God near'.[7] Rod Garner speaks about the prologue of John's

Gospel as having the ability to achieve this. 'The wisdom of the prologue lies in its capacity to bring about a shift in our imagination that can give birth to a deeper love.'[8] We are also called to speak of the deepest things while leaving on one side pious and unnecessary language and using well the gifts of silence and prayer.

Leadership is about discerning where the wisdom of God is residing in the people we meet and minister to, both within and outside our ecclesial communities. Like Simeon and Anna, at times we watch and wait for this to emerge. Wise leadership means taking time to listen, often to several voices of 'deep' that we have learned to trust, people like Don who show us something of what it means to be spiritually mature, through faithful living and humble serving, with a genuine sense of their own self-unimportance. This means that we live perpetually open to new horizons of God's activity in a changing church environment and society. Within such living there should always remain a willingness to be obedient to contribute in some way, to take up our cross and be a disciple, along with others in our community. Christopher Cocksworth talks about the variety of different kinds of wisdom:

> There will be all sorts of evidence of wisdom in a Christian community and yet there may be times when new perspectives are given to particular people. This is the wisdom of the *charismata*, the charisms of Christ, the gifts of the Spirit. The wise believer, especially the wise leader, will seek after these sorts of in-breakings and unfoldings of wisdom from God that enable us to see situations with a surprising clarity and to make decisions that bear the stamp of the Spirit of Christ.[9]

A further and final understanding of 'deep' moves away from our first idea, that wisdom can be discovered in the very stuff of life itself, in what is 'known' and experienced. In contrast, a profound wisdom can come from the acknowledgement that the gateway to God is a journey into the 'unknown'. One of the founding moments of faith in the history of the Hebrew people is when God gives Moses not an easily accessible name but the cryptic description, 'I Am Who I Am'. Moses, as leader, has to contend with not knowing himself who God is and also has to relate this back to the people who are desperate to understand God's nature. This may sound familiar to certain questions asked of Christian leadership today; people look to us to tell them who God is, how he operates and where he is in people's lives. Even for Moses, one of the founding fathers of the faith, God refuses to show his glory. God says, 'I will make all my goodness pass before you and you shall not see my face.'

Melvyn Matthews, in his book *Awake to God*, comments that there is something authentic about living within the unknown mystery of the divine that connects with a postmodern consciousness that does not necessarily sit easily with black-and-white statements of faith. This is a biblical faith, he says, which faces the unknowns of existence, including even the apparent absence of God, and understands the asking of questions, perhaps particular kinds of questions, as a characteristic of wisdom itself. And perhaps it is the kind of questions we ask, ones that 'prompt wonder, ones that occasionally keep us awake at night or even require us to re-evaluate our lives and priorities'.[10] Contemporary theologians Rob Bell and Robin Meyers have identified this new way of living and believing as a return to an ancient understanding of the faith that experiences the life of God more as a movement. Brian McLaren writes:

> Growing numbers of us believe that we are in the early stages of a new movement of emergence, pulsing with danger and promise. In this catalytic period, all our spiritual traditions will be challenged and all will change – some negatively and reactively, tightening like angry fists, and others positively and constructively, opening like extended arms . . . faith was never intended to be a destination, a status, a holding tank or a warehouse. Instead, it was to be a road, a path, a way out of the old and destructive patterns into new and creative ones.[11]

And like all the best walks, the adventure is discovering that the mapped-out route is unpredictably different from what we are expecting.

The recent brilliant film *Calvary* shows the life of a Roman Catholic priest in a claustrophobic rural community in Ireland. The priest, Father James, is on the receiving end of spitefulness and bitterness from members of his flock, which includes people abused by former priests and others who remain cynical to the claims of faith in a contemporary world. Wisdom is shown in James' ability to simply absorb this vitriol, well aware of the darkness not only in terms of evil but also in many of his parish who no longer accept the easy platitudes of past religion. Also aware of the demise of the traditional forms of church, he faithfully and lovingly continues amid much goading, until he eventually becomes the scapegoat of many damaged pasts, and this culminates in his murder. Some, however, recognize what he unselfconsciously communicates, refusing to give in to easy answers about the nature of God.

For the fourteenth-century mystic known as Meister Eckhart, God was a seemingly immense reality, beyond human comprehension. For Eckhart, God could be described in terms of emptiness, nothingness, wilderness, darkness and silence – in other words, language that suggests our human incapacity to comprehend who he is. By doing this Eckhart was not denying the existence of God but rather recognizing that compared to us God is a totally *other* being. The implication of this (known as the 'negative way') is that we should never stop our discussions about God and who he is merely because God cannot be defined or constricted by the limits of our semantics and language. The only other response is silence, but a silence that is reverent and wonder-inspired. Within Eckhart's theology is a sense that as humans we are always unfinished, never a static or completed entity. This sense of the unfinished means that we have the capability to be open to the transcendent at every stage of life. Eckhart was a controversial thinker in his day, believing that the human soul always has the potential for growing into the mystery of God in an attitude of openness. His aim for his listeners was to recognize the ultimate reality that is God – the unknown – which in turn recognizes the unknown and mysterious beauty within ourselves.

There is a wisdom here – wisdom that tells us to recognize that none of us can ever be sure about the nature and purpose of God, however much we like to think we hold all the definitive answers. This acknowledgement that Eckhart brought to the fourteenth century proved a refreshing counterbalance to the desire for over-zealous Christians to vehemently construct God in their own image, an image that for some people proved frightening. It is perhaps the same in our own church today. This theology enables those who seek and search to be affirmed in the mystery of the 'non-answer' that proves their actual experience of God. There is a detachment yet also wise honesty in such an emphasis on the dark unknowing of the person and presence of God. Melvyn Matthews puts it succinctly: 'Eckhart urges his Christian hearers to live without a "why" because the universe is within the gratuitous outpouring of God's constant spookiness.'[12]

Matthews points out that contemporary Christians often do experience God in negative terms but they lack the vocabulary to express this, while clergy may lack the mystical awareness of the importance of such experience and remain unable to articulate it positively. Many people, he says, remain alienated from the Church because of the contemporary emphasis on the importance of experiencing Jesus, and they are therefore not affirmed in the more mystical experience of 'unknowing' as has been described. The task for leaders – the wise task – is to try to dispense with the idea that infiltrates our spirituality today, that of 'progress', as we rather abandon ourselves into the velvet darkness of God. We must rediscover that to approach God in a similar way is part of our religious heritage.

The wisdom that is the result of this is about discovering a different and potentially more freeing understanding of who God is, an understanding that God is the source of all being rather than simply the object of belief, not, perhaps, to be endlessly discussed and examined but recognized as the source of all life. In fact, it is we ourselves who become the known (as opposed to the know-*er*) as we are increasingly made aware of the depth of God's love for us. Thomas Merton describes a trip out from his monastery. In the middle of a busy shopping arcade, with people milling about him, he is suddenly overwhelmed by the love God has for all humanity, which he too feels in that moment. There is something here about a wise and intuitive awareness of a power that unifies and joins every aspect of human life together.

To grow towards wisdom, then, is to live a life and practise a ministry that approaches potentially all experiences and all people as phenomena that contain God's presence at a multitude of differing levels. 'Deep' happens when we are able to wrestle with even the hard things and difficult people and learn from them. 'Deep' happens when we can reclaim and retain the beauty and redemption of God when all around others might see ugly crassness. A life in wisdom means living within an attitude of childlike exploration, of humility and service, of seeing the world through God's eyes and not being swayed by the damaging attitudes of those who do not see it this way at all. Wisdom is something that slowly matures, growing when we surround ourselves with those who immerse themselves 'in God'. It is something that requires a sense of philosophical and holy perspective as well as a defiant sense of humour. There can be the tendency to drink good wine far too quickly, with the result that we do not savour it, we do not understand the complexity of its flavours and perhaps do not remember the occasion of drinking it. Like bulls in china shops, we have the tendency to rampage through our life at speed through the everyday, rather than extracting the learning and the preciousness from within it.

Deep in practice

Individual

- Think back over the past week. What is the most significant thing that has happened to you, or has made you sit up and take notice of something or someone? Reflect on this more than you might otherwise have done in the past. If you are unused to reflecting on events in your own life, as well as in the life of the world, then try to make this a regular practice. Think beyond this to situations where the presence of God has or maybe hasn't been, and also think about what you are learning from such reflections. How might you take these further?

- Think about *the whole of your life* in the light of the above exercise. Potentially you could map out the significant times and events, and note why they were so. This exercise is given to all ordinands in my diocese, to chart the significant 'God-moments', particularly for people in whom you are trying to discern God's activity in past and present, and also identifying experiences that are nudging them into a new future. But for us all this can help in reflecting on the ongoing presence of God and developing the knowledge that every life is contained in the life of God.

- Develop practices that will enable you to grow into a person of wisdom and depth. Read good-quality novels (and perhaps savour them), and books on theology and spirituality that make you feel alive and excited when you read them; watch films and think about the themes within them; read and study your Bible more; reflect on your travel experiences. Avoid people who talk too much, and if that's you then try to use your words more sparingly. With this you may find more time for silence in your life.

- Reflect on how to deal with the problematic situations and people in your life and think about how you could deal with these more positively, honestly and in ways that prove life-giving to others.
- If you had to rewrite the ten commandments for living a wise Christian life, what would they be? Back them up biblically.
- Identify who the wise people have been in your past and who they are in the present. What is it that distinguishes the people you just want to 'be around'?

Corporate

- Run a simple study course, discussion group or sermon series on 'What does it mean to be a person of depth and wisdom in the world today?' With this also comes the question 'Why is this important?' Look at the Wisdom literature in the Bible. It can be found in the Genesis creation stories, in Proverbs and throughout the Psalms, in Job and in the accounts of King Solomon's life in 1 Kings. Ecclesiastes helpfully explores a very contemporary problem – that life is worthless and ultimately feels meaningless if the love and respect for God is not a factor in it. For an overview see Christopher Cocksworth's booklet *Wisdom: The Spirit's Gift.*
- Although they are not always easy to read, and may take some effort on the leader's part, decide to study one of the fourteenth-century mystics such as Julian of Norwich; or a more recent person of wisdom and holiness like Thomas Merton.
- Members of the clergy might usefully try to identify who the wise people are in your own congregation or work circles. Reflect on what it is about them that sets them apart

from others? If you can, spend more time with them in some way.

- It's difficult when we are juggling so much, but try to make a small commitment to dispensing with something that is unnecessary in your church's life; as an alternative, lead others in something that will develop and deepen them as people who are close to God.

8

Link

Loving interconnection

———◦——

The whole idea of compassion is based on a keen awareness of the interdependence of all these living beings, which are all part of one another and all involved in one another.

(Thomas Merton)

I live with my Jewish neighbour, I eat with my Muslim friend, I listen with the Quaker who sits and listens with me, and I slowly learn about the religions of South East Asia . . . I can and do remain a Christian, but my body is continually mapped onto other bodies . . . (Graham Ward, *Cities of God*)[1]

The five-star Taj Mahal Palace Hotel in Mumbai employs over 1,500 staff. With over 500 rooms and luxury suites it inevitably attracts the world's great and good. The 2014 BBC series *Hotel India* showed a snapshot of the variety of life in this most complex and vibrant of places. Here hospitality is taken to the extreme; in a 'can do' culture typical of India, guests feel that they are encountering a little bit of heaven as they are treated to immaculate bedrooms and attentiveness to the point of obsession from the staff. Here the 'guest is God', particularly when that guest is paying for it handsomely.

Viewers were taken on a journey up into the heights of luxury enjoyed by guests and down into the hard lives of those who serve, some of whom endure a two-hour journey to work. The striking element was the way that all operations and all people are inextricably bound up together. Here is a genuine, aspirational, accommodating and respectful 'family', linked by common ideals and tasks. Standards are high, and the staff with clout continually challenge those beneath them, but the lives of the least seem known and cared for. During the three-day siege of the hotel in the 2008 terrorist attack on Mumbai many of the kitchen staff sacrificially cared for the guests, hiding them in the kitchen and helping them to escape, sometimes at the cost of their own lives. This flexible family which ebbs and flows constantly with staff and guests is intrinsically and powerfully connected like the toughened steel of an industrial chain.

No one can live for even one day without acknowledging that they are linked in some way to others. Ironically in a western culture that tells us that to be successful we need to be independent and self-sufficient, a culture that communicates the subconscious message that we have 'moved on' from God, life seems more interconnected than ever. We are linked with others by instant messaging and Instagram, to those in our immediate circle of friends as well as to people far away, simply through the food we buy in the supermarkets. We cannot exist in any way in isolation. We are connected to thousands and millions of other people in our world by both visible and invisible strands. We have become so sophisticated that many of these links in our life-chain are not even recognized or acknowledged by us at all. *Hotel India* portrayed a significant aspect of our human and spiritual condition, in that those living within its walls needed one another for the whole crazy enterprise to function and flourish. Wages aside, people worked against the odds to serve others and relationships of appreciation and respect have been built up over years between guests and workers.

Our lives are full of links with others – positive and negative, tentative and established, immediate as well as anonymous. The Christian faith considers such linking with each other as both an opportunity and a command to love as the ultimate and underlying dynamic of everything we do. The mystical tradition recognizes and intuitively senses the magnitude of God's love which pervades and fills every atom and inch of the universe. Link is not only a recognition but a desire to make connections with others, however strangely different they feel, in order to find some common ground with which to create relationship, whether temporal or developing. Link is the phone call to a friend across the ocean; it is responding to the person wanting to chat on the train. Link is cultivating a spirit of anti-dismissiveness of all people, particularly those who are considered problematic and painful to deal with. Link means carrying within ourselves an ever open attitude that speaks of connection rather than fear and defence. Link runs against the flow of my own introverted desire to run or to judge. And link can probably only happen from a deep-seated, worked-through knowledge that we are loved first, and that love is the glue that connects everything together, whether good, bad, weird or 'other'.

In a context of social and religious uncertainty perhaps akin to our own, Julian of Norwich wrote her extraordinary treatise on the love of God, the *Showings*, in 1373; it was expanded at some point during the 1390s. Experiencing a life-threatening illness and believing herself to be nearing the end of her earthly life, this young woman saw a vision of a bleeding crucifix which stimulated a series of 16 'revelations of love' which she describes in intense language. The book in essence is a reflection about how human people relate to God and how God relates to us. Through her suffering, Julian pleads with God for three things, described in the language of the 'wound' – a deep-seated sorrow for sin, loving compassion, and a longing to be tuned in to what God really wants in the world. At the time her yearning to be joined to the sufferings of Christ marked a shift in how people understood God. Hers was not a powerful, objective hero-God but one who suffered because of love. For Julian this meant that she was able to enter more fully into the Passion of Jesus and to experience the effects of this in her life. Grace Jantzen comments:

> Julian was not praying for visions for their own sakes, or for strange spiritual or physical occurrences to gratify religious mania. She was praying rather for greater integration, compassion and generosity; and it seemed to her that these means would enable her to develop them.[2]

To our twenty-first-century imaginations, visions of bleeding crucifixes sound like the macabre spirituality of a typical horror movie my teenage daughter might watch rather than a genuine experience of a God who lives. But Julian's vision was her way into understanding in depth the immensity of the implications of an interpersonal Trinitarian God who seeks to relate to humanity at every level, and the complexity of a love that continues to be part of human experience throughout history. Her vision is described with language of total inclusivity and interrelatedness – of drawing all things together. She calls God 'Mother', which stems from her theology of the Trinity – a metaphor for the all-embracing love of God, which arguably culminates in her description of the hazelnut, its vulnerability encased in a shell as each human person is wrapped or sheltered in the love of God. At the end comes the phrase that has become the mantra widely associated with her spirituality; she expresses her firm belief that God's goodness fills all of his creatures: 'All shall be well and all manner of thing shall be well' – a remarkable confidence that ultimately, although wars and great evil rage, love is the all-powerful force at work and it will bring peace.

To live a prayerful life, for Julian, is to perceive this sense of the immensity of God's love and to be so overwhelmed by it that it transforms us enough to potentially change the way we approach and regard others. Melvyn Matthews puts it succinctly:

The Trinity is not a puzzle to be understood but a mystery which envelops all things and in which we and all things live and come awake. Here there is a sense of how all things are involved in God, everything is integrated, which we find throughout Julian's text and which is a particular characteristic of much post-modern theological reflection.[3]

As followers of Jesus trying to live in holiness, the idea of 'link' is about us *sensing* this at every opportunity, which may involve an act of will as well as of heart. Link is essentially about believing this in our innermost being and allowing love to transform us. It is also about stepping out of the comfort zones of ourselves and into the territory of someone else's soul. Link is fundamentally 'what it says on the tin': searching and striving to make links with other people, who on the surface may have nothing in common with us. I have found that when I approach situations within such a framework of love, with this mindset, then God opens up amazing possibilities. Being part of a Christian community can be the place where this is felt, even if only a little, and learnt, a place where we recognize the potential emptiness within ourselves that we may yearn to fill with love, acceptance and fellowship. Church can become the place where we can relearn how to link ourselves with others who feel disturbingly different from us yet who are linked by a common journey as well as an awareness of the mystery of God.

In our church we are lucky enough to have large and frequent baptism services. Often we have two families at one service, sometimes three. Occasionally, when I am tired and harried by the fact that this is already my third service of the day, and by a congregation (which feels like an audience) of gum-chewing, texting, chatting people who understand nothing about the culture of church, internally a struggle goes on between my soul and God. My inner, honest dialogue sometimes sounds like this: 'They don't "get" what this service is about, they think I'm crazy, what is the point because no one comes back,' which battles with: 'Jesus would look at these folk with utter and all-consuming love, he would see this as an opportunity for the Holy Spirit to be felt and for people to be transformed even just a little – and so must I.'

Ministry lived with this sense of the depth of God's love means that we are constantly looking for the links, for the common denominators, for bridges to be built, for interest to be shared within our common humanity. When this is achieved then the whispers of God begin to be heard and felt and they are powerful beyond measure. As Christians, 'others' – any others – will know us because of the loving graciousness that we show to other people, as well as the interest we take in their lives. It concerns me that many people I meet seem to not possess, or have lost, the simple ability to take an interest in the lives of other people. We must be different from this.

Living and looking for the 'link' also changes our perception of prayer and how it expresses itself. Prayer becomes less a petition-like practice and more of a continuous attention to the presence of God, a way of identifying the hidden gems or the painful shards buried within people. It means that we make the effort to be interested in others and give them time, even a little, and by doing this we show that we care and that they matter, both to us and to God. It transforms the way we do everything and how we approach ministry. When link becomes the starting point for our relationships then our guarded encounters have the potential to surprise us away from judgemental first impressions to become something much more spirit-led, unpredictable, intimate and even costly.

The 2014 film *Pride* is inspired by the true story of the link made between a group of gay and lesbian activists and a small Welsh mining community in the Dulais Valley caught in the middle of the 1984 miners' strike. Seeing the hardship suffered by the miners on television, a young gay rights activist, Mark Ashton, whips up support among his community to raise funds for the miners and their families. When the group visits the

conservative rural community they are met initially by a perhaps expected attitude of prejudice from a village that has not
encountered much 'difference' in all its history. But eventually
most are won over by Mark's insistence that these two apparently polar-opposite communities are linked by their common
struggle, primarily through a sense of powerlessness. The immense
and sacrificial love shown by the activists to the miners and
their families is moving. Throughout the film the Severn Bridge,
together with the image of a human handshake, seeks to emphasize this idea of the interconnection, which can be forged and
grow if genuine love underpins it. Link is the belief that stepping
away from our own concerns towards those who need help
transforms the world as well as ourselves. The film ends with
busloads of miners arriving unexpectedly to support a Gay
Pride march.

What the film communicates is that to link with others who
are different from us often takes effort and perseverance, when
it would be easy to turn away. At various points in the film
some members of the Dulais community say that they do not
want to accept money from such a group of controversial strangers. But the 'gays', as they affectionately become known, remain
undeterred, until the link is so strong that members of both
communities realize with crystal clarity that they have become
genuine friends. For us, then, as people who claim to follow a
God of love, this must go without saying. Living prayerfully is
about modelling seeking a connection with those we meet and
those in church as well. Our natural inclination is to gravitate
to people who might be the same personality types as ourselves.
Link challenges us to push through the boundaries of familiarity
and feeling comfortable, to seek to establish relationships with
those who are challenging, tiring, or from a completely different social background or different age group and generation.
I constantly get asked in my own congregation what the young
people 'would like', or whether there is anyone younger who
would take on a particular task. My answer is usually, 'Well,

why don't you ask them yourself?' or even better, 'If you don't know them then get to know them.'

A recent article in the *Church Times* reflects on how this kind of engagement happens in public places, where brave steps are tentatively initiated by Christian ministry being offered to strangers. Jonny Walker, founding director of the Keep Streets Live Campaign, speaks about bringing his music to the street, not self-consciously to spread the gospel but simply to enrich the experience of those places where he chooses to play. He speaks about it being 'really important to engage with people who don't even realize that they are your audience'.[4] With this is the idea that in all our dealings with others our task is to engage and link through the mutual love that cascades through the channels of our existence in myriad ways. Music, like many art forms, is a way of making connections that communicates the shared creativity of God. Thomas Merton, in *No Man is an Island*, writes about a love that can only be ours when it is given away:

> There is no end to the sharing of love, and, therefore, the poten-
> tial happiness of such love is without limit. Infinite sharing is
> the law of God's inner life. He has made the sharing of ourselves
> the law of our *own* being, so that it is in loving that we best
> love ourselves.[5]

He goes on to say that this only works when love is shared freely and with a right attitude. Our destiny is to love as Jesus loved – a man who had a relatively small circle of friends yet loved sacrificially. While we cannot be God we can recognize in an openness of heart that, 'The lives of all we meet and know are woven into our own destiny, together with the lives of many we shall never know on earth.'[6]

In a different continent, Sara Miles, in *City of God: Faith in the Streets*, describes one extraordinary day when she and some colleagues took the Ash Wednesday service out into the streets of San Francisco in an attempt to connect people with this deeply significant of days in the Christian year. Complete with Brazilian drummers, incense and copal to bless the four directions of the world, Sarah's group managed to connect with everyone from grandmothers to heroin addicts in this 'public square', through the power of symbol and loving human encounter. She describes the day with earthy sacredness:

> I knelt. I bent over and pressed my forehead to the sidewalk – the whole rush of this neighbourhood, its crazy beauty and apparent hopelessness, flooding my heart. I'd eaten tacos, chatted with beggars and laughed with friends on this holy ground. 'Lord,' I whispered, 'have mercy.'[7]

One of Miles' companions, Kelsey, makes a poignant comment on the experience, after imprinting the sign of the cross on a variety of people from teenagers to bar tenders. She comments, 'I'm glad to be here because I need to be with people who aren't like me. I just want – I don't know, I want to feel connected to them in another way, let my little chatting, judging, evaluating mind quieten down and just be with human beings.' For Miles, as for us, this is the point – the place of encounter between our essential un-ego selves, the place where we put aside all the mental stuff that gets in the way of simply loving others. She sums it up beautifully: 'That's exactly what people in the Mission had done for me. And in each moment of encounter – brief, intense, unpredictable – God's presence flared out, as if my hand and a stranger's face became, together, the tent of meeting.'

Julian of Norwich's longer adaptation of *Showings* describes a similar radical understanding of a God who is so consumed with love for the world that he is entirely without wrath. One of Julian's concerns is how this impassioned belief can become reconciled in a world that often does not behave as though this were true. One thing we have inherited from Julian's spirituality is the belief that whenever one person behaves and cultivates such an attitude then everything that is not right with the world is redeemed by love – in that moment. This is a hugely powerful notion, which finds its origins in the theology of the cross. This might feel like an implausible, maybe inconceivable interpretation of the power of love, but it nevertheless offers individual people a way of behaving that lends itself to the transformation of themselves and others.

Thomas Traherne, the seventeenth-century mystical writer, explores something of this idea but from a different perspective. He believed in the interconnectedness of all things, that life is lived within an 'enhanced colour' described as joy. Traherne's spirituality is the welcoming and embracing of all things. He took a great interest in the scientific discoveries of his day but rather than approaching these defensively he enlarged his theology accordingly so that his faith was never diametrically opposed to the new discoveries of science.

This incarnational and steeped joy exists between God and creation, between God and us, and between ourselves and others. Indeed the three are deeply intertwined and Traherne writes that our own need for love and 'link' is a mirror of God's need for *us* to reciprocate such a love:

> This is very strange that God should want. For in him is the fullness of Blessedness. He overfloweth eternally . . . He is from all eternity full of want . . . want is the fountain of his fullness. Want in God is treasure to us. For had there been no need He would not have created the world, nor made us, nor manifested his wisdom . . . But he wanted Angels and Men, Images, Companions: and these he had from all eternity.[8]

He rationalizes that what God wants we must want in return. For Traherne, it is because God loves us and links himself to us that we inherently feel this draw, this return too. And it is because of Jesus and his death on the cross that humanity is able to be linked to this love. The life, death and resurrection of Christ makes 'link' an eternal possibility. Traherne's spirituality in essence belongs to the cataphatic strand of mysticism, which understands that all things are needful of one another and interconnected, that the substance and method of divine love is so mind-blowing that we sometimes cannot grasp the immensity of it fully. Here is a way of relating to God that is also profoundly un-egotistical, one that accepts that all life is not only gift but part of something mysteriously greater than ourselves.

In the writings of Julian of Norwich and Thomas Traherne there is the acknowledgement that being a faithful and prayerful person is simply understanding that our lives, our beings, are already enveloped in the being of God, that there is already a sense of the life of God within them, found by belonging in relationship rather than asserting individual needs and rights. They speak of a spirituality that is participative and that insists that there is no distinction between what we might call 'religious' awareness and the ordinary everyday experiences of life. There is no 'secular' and 'religious' but rather a relearning to see and live life with renewed awareness that the mystical flows through it for those with eyes open enough to see and hearts wide enough to love much. It is about re-seeing something that is already before us like a shimmering rainbow. Matthews sums this up well: 'Involved in this reawakening is a real self-forgetfulness, a loosening of the ties between us and our ego-selves so that identity is found by belonging in relationship rather than by asserting individual rights and needs.'[9]

On holiday in small-town Spain this year we hit fiesta season. Naturally aided by days of extended sunshine my family sat in the public square watching eccentric local customs, the saints of the locality (St Michael and St Rocque) being paraded around the town, a carnival and street performers and the bizarre but contagious 'foam party' where a foam machine bathed the square with a giant bath of detergent. Visitors and residents alike dived in to join together in this wet and happily demented exuberance. In a society of health and safety, child protection and horror stories of treachery of all kinds, our natural inclination to discover a common humanity with others is, at this time in human history, in danger of being squashed and suffocated. But the gift of God urges us ever forwards, to join in, to make links and connections, to celebrate our humanity both with known and unknown others, enabling us to feel the divine strength and the challenge and spontaneity of a God who tells us that ultimately we are never, ever alone.

Link in practice

Individual

- Think about someone you believe you have nothing in common with and try to get to know them, looking for things that connect you as human people.
- Reflect on one way your life connects with people locally, nationally and internationally. Make time to pray for them even if you don't know them. Think about how your actions have an impact upon those who make these connections possible and what you could do that could potentially improve the life of someone who remains anonymous to you (for example, you don't know the people who produce the bananas you buy but you could help someone by buying Fairtrade).
- Live one day next week talking to more people than you might otherwise do and strive to find connections, perhaps by reflecting on the encounters in retrospect.
- When you are next in a situation where you are in danger of being rude, impatient, dismissive or judgemental about another person, stop and think yourself into their humanity. Challenge yourself to make mental links between you and them.
- If you have a friend who is very different from you, find opportunities to talk about this as a witness to the idea of link, especially with people who might find this idea challenging.

Corporate

- Find ways in your worship and church life for there to be regular interaction between people who are different from one another in your community. This might be about encouraging home and study groups to include people of different backgrounds and age groups rather than people just sticking with their friends. Lead an act of worship/sermon slot where members of your congregation tell stories about the links they have with people locally, nationally and internationally and how they might experience the life of God within these.

- Find biblical passages about people discovering the presence and purpose of God through interacting with people who are different from them – the Gospels are full of them!

- Do some serious work on your welcome policy. Think about one area in your community where more links could be made between the church and that group or institution. How does your church tangibly express love for its members, and for those who are not a regular part of its number?

9

Shed

Letting go and letting grow

———◆◆———

Life today is fast paced, stressed and materialistic. We need to declutter our hearts, our workloads, and our homes to counter the effects. (Andrew Barton, *Decluttering*)[1]

The things you own end up owning you.
(Tyler Durden in *Fight Club*)

Let come what comes, let go what goes. See what remains.
(Ramana Maharashi)

In 2001 the British conceptual artist Michael Landy organized a piece of performance art called *Breakdown*. Over a two-week period, in a redundant C&A store, a moving, airport-like baggage carousel processed, disassembled, shredded and granulated each of his 7,227 possessions. Like many artists, Landy was more interested in the process than the end result, although he recognized that among his possessions were items of both monetary and sentimental value. According to the artist, the process worked best when it resonated with members of the public, becoming a shared experience as people peered into the trays and made a mental inventory of how much they themselves had accumulated, asking questions of their lifestyle choices.

Landy's intention was not to moralize or lambast people for being consumers, however. He recognized that working hard to acquire things that we are proud of and give us identity is part of a fairly normative approach to life lived in a western culture. For him the installation was more a comment on our consumerist tendencies than a reflection stemming from a specifically spiritual standpoint. But his friend and colleague, Dave Nutt, a practising Buddhist and the mechanic who took Landy's Saab car apart, interpreted the piece from a different perspective, as did many people of faith who viewed it. One thing that delighted the artist was the overwhelmingly positive response, as though the radicalness of what was happening both freed and echoed with people and the possessive habits that build up over a lifetime.

Another of Landy's projects, *Art Bin*, has strong connections with *Breakdown*. In 2010 in the South London Gallery an enormous transparent bin was erected as 'a monument to failure' – the words the artist used describing the piece. He invited visual artists to throw away the works they considered to be failures. At the top of a flight of stairs, works of art were thrown into the 600 square metre bin. For many the process was twofold – the releasing of works that 'hadn't worked' well, and the simple dispensing with the clutter of 'stuff' we might keep by default.

Both *Breakdown* and *Art Bin* feel radical, subversive acts, perhaps also mysteriously refreshing. With both projects Landy seemed surprisingly unemotional. He commented that *Breakdown* was 'the best thing I have ever done'; he saw the destruction of his possessions as a creative rather than a nihilistic act. Similarly *Art Bin* suggests an inherent, even iconoclastic approach to creativity but the response of the many artists who participated was one of relief and release.

The point about performance art is that it is just this – a performance, a show, and yet a process that is undeniably real at the same time. Michael Landy really did crunch all his possessions, and artists really did throw their artwork in the bin. Art like this is active and moving, like every part of the process of human existence.

As Christian, priest and human being I live on a daily basis with the uncomfortable feeling that my life is filled to the brim with too much. Too many physical possessions, too much activity, too many activities I am involved in, things that have to get done, even things I actually want to do. Too many emails to clear, books to read, films to watch, bills to pay, people to care for, things to sort – simply too much for my individual brain to cope with. The more physical stuff we have, the more there is to insure, invest, clean, repair and worry about. Even in church, a place that should offer us space to think, pray, reflect and be challenged, I believe that for all sorts of reasons we tend to do and plan far too much these days. 'Shed', then, is an offering of a spirituality of subtraction as a way to live, pray and decrease in order to increase and expand our spirituality as a Christian person.

I have always found visiting the local recycling centre quite a spiritual experience. There is something deeply satisfying about getting rid of the excess in our domestic spaces in the knowledge that this will be dispensed with responsibly. These days we cannot just discard what we no longer want, but have to compartmentalize carefully, placing everything in the correct container to be dealt with accordingly. In his reflection on decluttering, Andrew Barton suggests that living with less and ridding ourselves of excess in every part of our life will make us powerful Christian witnesses. In today's post-Christendom society subconscious and persuasive voices encourage us to over-amass and to carve out our identity by what we own, what we do and what we achieve. Barton suggests that the answer lies in us divesting of the 'too much' in our lives, be these ideas, events or physical possessions, because a life that becomes too full reduces how effectively we live. He advocates a regular 'clearing out' of life, believing that this is a prayerful discipline. But it is also about approaching such a process with a sensitive and careful attitude, just as we would recycle our unwanted possessions with a responsible attitude. He recognizes that getting rid of things can be about letting go because of the associations our possessions or roles have for us. Dispensing with in this sense is sometimes about bereavement and it is vital that we are left with the things that are really important to us. These might be objects given to us as gifts, or roles and interests that we have worked hard to achieve, which gather an emotional sense of importance. He suggests practical ways to approach a 'spirituality of dispensing' that is not about a forced austerity but more about an opening up of physical, emotional and spiritual space where we can have more room for God, others and ourselves in every part of our existence.

The Bible is full of stories of the wisdom of shedding, which is sometimes associated with the idea of purging. In the Old Testament material possessions (often in the form of people and animals) may be understood as a blessing from God, but are also connected with people 'on the move', people whose primary focus, like Abraham himself, is on establishing God's promised land for the future of others. But throughout the Bible riches come as an inevitable distraction to those in power. In the New Testament Jesus' challenge to the rich young man in Mark 10 is well known; his instruction to sell all he has and give to the poor flattens every ounce of mock virtuosity in the man's apparent righteousness. It is a warning that if acquisitiveness and a life of yearning and cramming gets the better of us then we will become enemies of the kingdom. Zacchaeus, on the other hand, is championed by Jesus because of his complete turnaround and conversional attitude to his way of wealthy living. Indeed, all through the Gospels the people with the least seem to have more space, more room to understand the message of the radical love of God.

In Luke 9, Jesus famously sends out the disciples, stressing: 'Take nothing for your journey, no staff, nor bag, nor bread, nor money – not even an extra tunic.' In *Mission-Shaped Spirituality*, Susan Hope suggests that the reason for this was twofold. First, it meant that those who travelled had to trust in God's provision; second, the need for physical things like food and shelter automatically propelled the disciples to search out others, to form relationships with strangers.[2] We might not be called to such a radical calling, but this suggests that the less we have the more likely we will be to need the help of others, encouraging the dynamic of God to work, perhaps through hospitality. We might also get used to living with the dynamism of the present moment, responding to the now rather than the anxiety of the future that acquisitiveness often brings. This issue is therefore crucially bound up with freedom. Living prayerfully and missionally, Hope says, is about 'an invitation to "change our gods"'. There is something powerful and compelling about living in a minimal way, living with things that are beautiful as well as personal but in a way that is not physically or emotionally cluttered and promotes a life lived with room to offer hospitality to others – a big theme for the early Christian communities of the New Testament. As we know, the early believers often lived in homes with the kind of fluidity discussed in Chapter 3 on Flux; their houses were open to any who might come as itinerant evangelists, and they often pooled their resources to help one another and those who were struggling.

My son has a pet corn snake. Every six to eight weeks the snake's bright orange markings begin to look lacklustre and muted. We recognize this now as the snake being near to shedding his skin, and once this has happened his stunning vibrancy returns. The point is that we too can become dull when our lives are overly full – either from material things or when we are too busy. For it is then that we become so stressed with our own concerns that even being with God feels like another thing we have to fit in, and it seems nigh impossible to reserve space for the unpredictable. Busyness in particular can produce a subtle sense of our own importance, which is sometimes oppressive to others whose lives are perhaps not quite so full. Like the snake, we are called to become bright again, to shed that which hinders us from living the sharp gospel message. So often this is about a sense of healing. The Gospels flow with stories of people whose lives are cluttered up with the things which prevent them flourishing and developing into the people God wants them to be. Luke 8 relates the time when Jesus encounters a madman in a graveyard, who is naked and possessed by so-called demonic forces that have left him raving for years. But both the man and the demons recognize the power of Jesus to rid him of what has become a destructive influence in his life. He begs Jesus to free him, and at Jesus' command the spirits leave the man and transfer themselves into a herd of pigs, who rush headlong over a cliff. Tough on the pigs, perhaps, but the result on the man is a new peacefulness and balance in his life.

The Hoarder Next Door is a Channel 4 documentary series about people who have collected a variety of possessions compulsively, sometimes for decades. Helped by the psychotherapist Stelios Kiosses and others, individuals are encouraged to free their homes from possessions that have built up over the years. In the process, viewers discover that these practices have often been generated by other unhealthy habits such as compulsive shopping, or that clinging onto things, often in terrible states of decay and disrepair, is about unresolved grief of one form or another. The habits of one person usually spill over to have a detrimental effect on partners and other family members and the clearing away of physical things involves a painful inner process, but if it is tackled sensitively and bravely the process ultimately brings new emotional life.

Some psychologists and theologians might state that behind the excess and the busyness of the overfull life is our inability to accept our own mortality. By concentrating on what we can achieve through career and possessions we temporarily quash the inevitable knowledge that all of us will one day die. The parable of the rich fool in Luke 12 – the farmer who builds larger and larger barns to store his ever-increasing crops – is a case in point. The farmer, although enjoying the apparent security of his produce, dies before he can enjoy or share any of it. His values are all wrong – he seems to have no friends or real fellowship with others, and so he dies alone, with his crops presumably rotting around him. Here is the story of someone who believes he has everything but actually has nothing. His life has been a life lived in self-deception dominated by what he can apparently achieve.

Lest I begin to sound sanctimonious I am a person who loves nice things, in particular good clothes and shoes. But underneath the compulsion to immerse and reward myself in shops that offer me an array of consumerist choice, I sense an ongoing urge to lessen and simplify my life, not just the things I own but the things I do. I am aware, for example, that I am simply too busy – happily so – but my life feels like a continuous scrambling to find snatches of time to tick off myriad tasks, pursuits and obligations, from the baking of the contributory church function cake to the demands of my job, as well as finding quality time to give to those I love, both near and far. Recently I gave up two roles I wasn't particularly enjoying, partly because I believe that these will be much better served by people with the necessary skills and background that I don't think I have. Once the initial wave of guilt dissipated I was pleased I made the decision. Perhaps it is personality dependent, but I also find it an increasingly uplifting experience to clear out the loft or other cluttered spaces, for I feel the pull for myself and my family to have just the things we need – things of quality that are used and enjoyed rather than lying in forgotten corners gathering dust. Having a family often makes it hard to live a physically minimalist life. My son has a penchant for collecting things and my teenage daughter loves clothes just like I do. Living a life that is busy and feels genuinely contributory to both Church and world is satisfying as long as there is also space enough for new things to arise and spontaneously happen.

But as Christians we can build in and promote among our own families and within our congregations a spirituality that kicks hard against the constant yearning to fill and collect. This proves a powerful antidote to the prevailing culture and, Andrew

Barton believes, becomes a more effective witness to those watching our faith than perhaps the average sermon. The challenge is to witness effectively and communicate the gospel much more through what we do as opposed to what we say; most people do not read the Bible much but they do observe what Christians do and how they live. He concludes:

> Christians can choose to mould their lives or be moulded by society around them. Society today stresses individuality which fosters in its turn a loneliness, a distrust of neighbour, a suspicion of the motives of others and consequently little hope or meaning on life. In turn there is a longing for spiritual reality in the face of confusion and *anomie*.[3]

In other words, as people who follow the simplicity and focused nature of Christ we have to suppress the urge to do what we might naturally want to do in line with the aspirations of our culture. The calling to live counterculturally is nevertheless being taken up by many individuals and communities the world over, whether by a determined choice or simply through necessity. A recent book records the history of the religious Community of the Transfiguration in Edinburgh and describes the ministry and witness of Roland Walls, radical priest and academic, who for over 50 years advocated and lived out an austere life of simplicity and contemplative prayer in a tin hut in the village of Roslin just outside Edinburgh.[4] As a child I visited this community, for my parents had become interested in it and its reputation had reached the far outpost of Cornwall hundreds of miles away. The vision of simple living coupled with a commitment to welcome vagrant people and those emotionally damaged by life generally was one that stayed with me, along with the fact that the lunch offered was only bread and peanut butter.

The calling of the desert fathers and mothers who lived in the sandy terrain of the Middle East from the third century onwards was to dispense with and work through all the things that hindered them in being filled with the presence of Jesus. Practising a Christ-like kenosis, or self-emptying, their aim was to create space for what was important. Some colourful stories exist of an extremity of behaviour that kept them away from even those who sought out their wisdom and time. One such character was the marvellous Symeon of Stylites, who lived in the fifth century and spent the majority of his life on top of a pillar situated north of Aleppo in Syria. As people sought out monks like Symeon, their pillars grew higher in the belief that God might be more likely to be encountered on a high place, an idea that followed many biblical precedents from Moses on Mount Sinai to the Transfiguration. In spite of this challenging and uncomfortable lifestyle choice, Symeon had many followers. There is something potent in stories like this about a way of living where there is literally no room for anything to impinge on a relationship with God – an unashamed desire to be stripped of all inessentials for the love of God alone.

The teachings we have inherited from the desert fathers and mothers became the foundation for many later religious monastic orders, many of whom lived persuasively with rules of life that encouraged self-discipline and riled against luxury. Their motivation was not self-denial for its own sake but a belief that it was grounded in Scripture. In her discussion of these ancient lives, Angela Ashwin says that such voluntary asceticism seems to have an oddly freeing effect upon us centuries later:

> if we stick with them, they may alert us to areas in our own lives where lesser things are preventing us from being our truest and best selves. They (the desert holy ones) believed that God would fill their emptiness with the presence of Christ. Even when their behaviour shocks us, these fools can inspire us to live in a simpler way and to be less bothered about trivia and more aware of each moment. A mind and heart less cluttered is a rare gift. It transforms our listening, our relationships, our praying and our life.[5]

Such statements speak into the unfolding and emergent enthusiasm for 'new monasticism', which calls people to re-envisage a sense of living in community. The movement seeks to recreate a moral and spiritual backdrop to life that enables people to live with Christian values that are distinctively different from the ones of materialism and individualism prevalent in our society today.

As priest I also have an inner conviction, lurking underneath the surge of surface energy, that our church lives are often filled with too much – too many meetings, projects and initiatives. Worse, we are often not very honest – all this activity may gloss over the fact that we are managing decline under the current system we understand as church. Lots of activity can be about genuine new life, but it can also hide our sense of fear and inadequacy at halting that decline, helping us to believe that we are involved in productive ventures. In our age of ecclesial reinvention it feels that we have arrived at an era that feels simultaneously releasing, exhilarating and disturbing – where our 'body' seems to be perpetually reassessing what it means to both 'be' and 'do' church. Years ago, the core ministry of preaching, presiding and pastoring seemed plenty for the vicar to do, but now our calling is to involve ourselves with much more, from church in the coffee shop to ambitious mission and discipleship schemes, often requiring months of strategic planning and the organization of a multitude of people. Those of us who lead feel the pressure to increase numbers and to keep reinventing ourselves in order to capture the religious imagination of an ever more diverse group of people from both secular and faith backgrounds.

But I am convinced that desperation and overwork can never be an answer to filling the gaps when we feel inadequate or overwhelmed. We are called first and foremost to be faithful as priests and Christians and to live, worship and practise ministry in a way that proves a marked contrast to how many live. We need to do fewer things but we need to do them well.

There needs to be focus, space to think and reassess, to pray and to listen to God, to others and to our contexts. Our church buildings should be places of peace and it helps if we can physically declutter them too, especially if the building has been left untouched for years. Our worship can have moments of stillness and silence, which will help to communicate the fact that our lives should have 'space' within them for those who participate. As Anglicans we understand liturgy, and mostly use this effectively, but we would perhaps do well to lessen our use of liturgical language at times, just as the holy ones before us used their speech sparingly. Currently many ideas are envisaged about what our Church will look like in ten, 20 or 100 years' time. Will the parish system still be operating, will we progress towards a minster model with a central church and a multitude of satellite worship centres, and will hundreds of smaller buildings have to close? Perhaps the answer to all these questions will be 'yes', but in the present there seems to be a deep desire among many clergy to dispense with unwanted 'clutter' in church life and to find ways for mission initiatives to be creative and manageable rather than overwhelming and unrealistic. We need to find ways of seeing fewer projects through to fruition (or even to fruitful first stage), rather than spreading ourselves thinly with multiple ventures. Look for the gaps in your local context, plan accordingly and stick to one or two projects or initiatives.

The act of praying itself also enables us to shed, to declutter our continuously whirring and highly sprung minds. Intercessions – praying for others – help us to offload the burdens we have trouble putting down, the crosses we carry, out of loving concern and worry for those we have responsibility for. We can mentally shed these from time to time and transfer them to the greatness of a mysterious God who we believe absorbs and copes with everything we cannot bear. Ancient exercises like the examen help us to 'unpack' the day we have lived, identifying the dark clouds as well as the silver linings, and moments where God has felt close and where he has felt absent. Physical stillness and meditative exercises can encourage us to discipline our minds, clearing them of current preoccupations and compulsions, so that we give God a freer passage to speak to us through his Spirit in the very depth of our personhood. Imaginative contemplation and learnt meditation techniques not only provide mental and spiritual decluttering but can help us to clear out other parts of our problematic lives, to air the rooms of our complex human nature. The Indian priest and writer Anthony de Mello devised some relevant specific exercises which have been helpful to me particularly in my work as spiritual director.[6] Of late and perhaps especially when people feel there is a barrier or blockage to praying, it is often the simplest techniques that enable spirituality to open up once more, for example simply imagining yourself in the same room as Christ or repeating a simple but age-old prayer such as the Jesus Prayer.

Shed is a potentially spiritual and physical dynamic process, one that we need to apply regularly to many parts of our life and leadership. It is the image of getting to the heart of the matter, of the sometimes necessary stripping away of the layers that get between us and loving others and loving God, like peeling away the unproductive parts of a plant that needs to rejuvenate itself by dispensing with what is hindering new growth.

Shed in practice

Individual

- Take time to declutter your home and working environment regularly. Don't clear too much at once; good decluttering involves making continuous decisions that often need to be approached with care and sometimes prayer. Think about how you might dispose of the things you don't need – recycling, the charity shop, people you know who might appreciate them; or can you sell the things you are throwing out? Be prepared to be ruthless – many people say that if you haven't worn or used something for a year (or perhaps two) then you probably won't again, but the same rule might not apply to everything, for example books or household objects. Try to assess whether something belonged to 'an era' in your life and now needs to go.

- Take a day every now and then to think and pray through how you use your time. Can you organize this better? Are there ways of opening up some space just as 'space', to use for prayer, or use more productively in another way? What activities can you dispense with or stop doing? Do you need to spend less time watching TV or clearing your emails and more time with your family, or alone? Think about what you could do without in your working life as well as domestic life.

- Diary in 'space' time – to rest, pray, walk, or learn how it feels to live in the 'empty' silence and stillness for 30 minutes. This can be daily, weekly, monthly, annually.

Corporate

- Put more silence and spiritual space time into worship. In our church we have introduced a significant two minutes of 'led' stillness before we begin our worship on a Sunday. The clergy person leading the service tells the congregation that there will be a period of silence before the service commences. People respect and, I think, enjoy this focus time. It has made a difference to the atmosphere of the entire service.

- Declutter the buildings you have responsibility for (but be aware of what you are allowed to change) and invest in new storage space if you can.

- Think about the ministry (perhaps meetings, or ventures) that you could now reduce your involvement in, or that needs either to end or be reconsidered.

10

Dream
Believing a future into being

———•◦•———

Faith communities live between memory and fulfilment, and what sustains us is our hope. The transgressive Spirit urges that our hope be unquenchable as we plunge deeper into the mystery of life.   (Mary Grey, *The Outrageous Pursuit of Hope*)

The message is clear: history belongs to the intercessors, who believe the future into being.
                    (Walter Wink, *Engaging the Powers*)[1]

Inwardly I groan. I've been drawn in yet again, against my better judgement. It's Saturday evening and another series of *The X Factor* shouts its glitziness from the TV. The contestants have been catapulted out of the greyness of their lives and made into temporary celebrities, the judges appear like gods overseeing a gently gladiatorial contest. What *is* so compelling about watching ordinary, often indefensible people live out their dream of becoming some kind of pop star? I've been through a whole journey with this programme. It's tempting to stand in supercilious judgement on a process that projects the often unlikely person to stardom only to squash their hopes of fame in a subsequent episode. Yet perhaps the reason it proves such compulsive viewing is because its underlying dynamic echoes the shared human desire we all carry to 'make our mark', to have the satisfaction of being involved in something worthwhile. Our society loves an underdog too, and wrapped around the talented few are often stories of brokenness, messed-up relationships or simply the lack of a chance to do something sensational. Perhaps what this series does is promote a vision (albeit a narrow one) of what it might mean to 'live the dream', and the public nature of its TV persona communicates a message to thousands that their own dreams might be possible too. Programmes such as *The X Factor* tell us, if we listen hard enough, that even though the world might be a tough environment to drive the dream through, people do not stop longing for them. This says something important about the human desire for a life that holds meaning, brings joy and contributes to the world, however individualistic this might seem.

Most of us have dreams and these continue throughout our lives, although they may change, or fade, or sometimes cry out so loud we can no longer ignore them. If asked about their 'dream', many people would probably be able to describe something, however wistfully, for that question often brings renewed animation to a bored or resigned humanity. As Christians we believe that our dreams move multilaterally – the spirit of God inspires us in our dreaming, and for our part our yearning and passion to do something amazing for God can only be lived out tangibly through our own hands and hearts. As *The X Factor* clearly demonstrates, dreaming is aspirational as well as vocational. Dreaming is about passion and inspiration, it's about determination and hope. Dreams produce passion but for dreams to connect with God's dreams to build an alternative world then such passion must be challenged to be channelled into hopeful dreams for the benefit of such a world. Bernard of Clairvaux said that the task of the Church is to help the world to move its passion into love in a way that truly reflects the vision and the love of God.

I have long loved the figures of the three magi in the Christmas narrative – the astrological men of probable wealth and vulnerable wisdom, who watched and looked upwards at the stars to discern an auspicious time for a momentous and divine event. Not a dream finely tuned and poised exactly, yet these men were alert to the presence of God breaking into the world in a new way. Why else would they leave the security of their lands to travel on a journey fraught with discomfort and probable danger? The magi follow the star and a divine dream that suggests to them that at some point in the history of the universe something of great significance will happen. They travel in trust and visionary hope; once arrived in front of the odd assortment of people, they lay down their gifts in front of Jesus, Saviour of the world. They then return from where they had come, God warning them, through the medium of the dream, to return by a different route. The magi were inspired, stirred to respond to a vision, a dream they believed was literally written in the stars. Dreams provide us with inner fire, fire to see things through, to set God's dreams in motion. The German New Testament scholar Gerd Theissen writes:

> A fire is kindled in those who are called by God. It is as though they were in love. In this state all doubts as to whether life and the world are meaningful have vanished. Life has a centre. Everything that is in contact with this centre is good. To be in the presence of the beloved is happiness in itself.[2]

People accused of being daydreamers are often individuals considered to be vacuous, a little 'spacey', people not rooted and grounded in the reality of whatever is perceived as the 'real world'. But the opposite is true for the genuine dreamers in our churches and communities, for dreaming is an uncomfortable thing. The God we believe in generates hope within us to live and believe a better and more beautiful world into being. As believers and pray-ers we often work counterculturally against a mindset of cynicism that tells us that there is no point attempting to live these out because ultimately nothing changes. Mike Leigh's film charting something of the life of J. M. W. Turner, the idiosyncratic artist, portrayed a gruff and grunting bear of a man whose personal life was often inwardly chaotic. Turner seemed to be oblivious to the etiquette expected of him as gentleman and painter; nevertheless he allowed his visionary talent to move the art of the day beyond the representational, elevating landscape painting to a new abstraction through his portrayal of light. In his day, Turner's reputation and gifts were subject to both adulation and ridicule from others, but his was, in spite of it all, an ardent and zealous dream world in paint. One message of the film is that for those who dare to share such a dream and despite all the flaws in human nature, the life of creativity can contribute to the history of the world.

Christian dreaming is a holistic activity, involving our heads and our hearts and also our guts – the guts that become the driving force required to change a dream from theory into practical reality. To dream is to take part in an age-old activity that sits on the boundary between the known and the unknown. Dreaming can show us our ordinary world through a bright technicolour lens, disturbing the complacency of our under- stood and perceived world, shaking us out of the known and challenging us to think about the parts of our lives God might be attempting to speak into. Dreaming, then, is punchy and dynamic; it connects with petitioning God for what has ultimately not yet come to pass, in our own lives and those of our communities and the world at large. Walter Wink, in his *Powers* trilogy, connects the idea of praying and dreaming. He suggests that prayer, and specifically intercession, is spir- itual defiance of what is, contrasted to what God has promised: 'Intercession visualizes an alternative future to the one appar- ently fated by the momentum of current contradictory forces. It infuses the air of a time yet to be, pricking the suffocating atmosphere of the present.'[3] His message is clear: history belongs to those who pray the future into being, however unlikely that dream might appear.[4] Hope envisages a future and then acts as if that future is now irresistible, thus helping to create the reality for which it longs. The future is not inevit- able or closed but open and pliable, even amid the most desolate of circumstances.

God works alongside our dreams, inspiring and enabling us to put them into practice through the power of his Spirit. Our dreams for the transformation of the world are thus a long way from being an escape from action, but become a means of focusing our energy into action. The Bible has many examples of God being the planter of dreams, and so we too can believe (with careful discernment) that it is God himself who is the dream implementer, giving us the yearning to pray and the passion to transform people and places that need love and powerful change. So when God initiates prayer within us and we respond and turn towards him, we choose to join his dream. Dreams have always had the capacity to move us on, often from one stage of life to another. A candidate for ordination I am currently seeing told me about a dream she felt was portentous for her life. The day before it, she had been in hospital with her mother who was seriously ill. During her long wait, she felt inspired to read some of the book of Acts. That night she had a dream which retained a sense of its significance in the morning. She dreamt of a transparent church, where there appeared to be no walls, where it was possible to see inside and those inside to see out. She spoke of a sense of her own calling as being in a place where she herself could act as a bridge, where she might 'sit between two worlds', enabling there to be a continuous and flowing two-way communication, a breaking down of barriers between those on the inside and those outside. This connects with her work pastoring an Iranian Christian community which currently meets in Liverpool Cathedral. She saw this as a powerful indication that God was trying to pull her ever onwards into a priestly and leadership role.[5]

Dreaming often suggests a phenomenon that is a subconscious, unconscious, perhaps even passive process which happens when we are asleep, out of control of the rational workings of our minds and bodies. Like the story above, on waking we are aware that dreams might be trying to say something to us, and we remember those that are especially significant; perhaps they occur at points in our lives when we are most pushed within our humanity. God speaks through dreams such as these but also speaks through dreams that become specific commands to individuals, perhaps to achieve something great, or simply to perpetuate a vision of hope in a bleak and vanquished world.

Brother Ramon SSF speaks of the biblical text as binding humankind together 'in a psychic and spiritual solidarity, where the prophets speak out of a situation of corporate personality. This is the context in which dreams can clearly impinge on the waking world, giving guidance and direction.'[6] The prophet Joel plays out precisely this theme. The people are suffering because of their apparent disobedience to God's call to live in righteousness. They are beset by locusts, crop failure and other miseries. But Joel proposes and presents a new vision to them and God shows mercy by restoring the fertility of the land. Joel 2.28 contains the famous dream of an extraordinary phenomenon where God's spirit will be poured liberally upon all:

> Then afterwards I will pour out my spirit on all flesh;
> your sons and daughters shall prophesy,
> your old men shall dream dreams,
> and your young men shall see visions.

The experience of dreaming featured throughout the life of Joseph, one of the Old Testament's most famous of dreamers. His boyhood dreams of pastoral scenes and celestial visions are both personal and cosmic, and proved relevant not only to him but to the people of God in their wider pilgrimage. As Joseph opened up his heart and mind to God's inspiration he also became open to the dreams of others even though this proved something of an uncomfortable vocation, with the likes of Pharaoh's wine steward and baker and then of Pharaoh himself. But if it had not been for Joseph's dreaming then his own people, including members of his immediate family, would not have been agitated enough to search out food in a country not their own, but instead would have starved to death in their homeland. In the New Testament Paul had several visions during his missionary career, dreams that sent him to preach in specific places to spread the news of God's kingdom. Other dreams and visions communicate an important message that God wants the world to hear. In Acts 10 God gives Peter a vision of animals lowered in a sheet, with a voice from heaven telling people to kill and eat beasts that were considered 'unclean' in Jewish law. This seemingly bizarre dream had massive consequences, then as now, with regards to how we understand the message of God's love as inclusive to everyone.

Mary Grey, in her book *The Outrageous Pursuit of Hope*, asks whether there is a specific dream for particular eras in the history of the world. She likens the experience of the exilic people of Israel with the loss of genuine homeland for many refugee peoples in the world who have had their livelihood and dreams obliterated, primarily by war. But she also talks about the loss of hope in a *fin de siècle* time in the West where individualism, competitiveness and a loss of corporate spirituality have persuasively created a culture of sapping apathy and sometimes despair that questions whether life holds any meaning at all. Her question is this: how can Christians sing the Lord's song in a culture where, like the Jews in Babylon, people of faith are often easily assimilated into secular culture – at times, we do not look so distinctively different from the atheist next door. Her answer lies in a subversive reading of the prophetic texts; she suggests that the radical Christian vision is to perpetuate hope when our individual or collective dreams are in danger of dying. She links this specifically with the power faith holds, and encourages the followers of Christ to be people who retain the energy and exuberance generated by a hopeful approach to life, which states passionately and firmly the belief that with God's power the world can be changed and infused with a new and more meaningful understanding of how to live.

But it can be frustrating, when we experience clergy and congregations who refuse to see the reality of a situation. And sometimes this is about not being able to look directly at the hardness of a painful situation, for example when a church building needs to close or a piece of ministry needs to cease. But there is something powerful and propelling about people who prayerfully persevere with their dream, their vision and their hope; like a fountain, dreams go from a high point to a low point, they are picked up and rechannelled. A city-centre church I worked at some years ago went through a huge re-ordering and reimagining of its interior. It was led by a visionary priest rector who refused to let the dream of what the church could offer be subsumed by a lack of money or politics, and included an ongoing arts project, a space for an eclectic and diverse congregation to meet and celebrate vibrant worship, a centre for health and healing and a café. The reordering was part of the bigger vision to completely reimagine the Bull Ring area of Birmingham. It cost the church more than £5 million, but the process of the 'dream', although bringing immense stretching and stress at times, brought creativity and a sense of the energy of God weaving throughout the funding and faculty applications. Working as the arts coordinator at the time, I liaised with several local youth groups to see what their dreams for a better city might be. These groups decorated the unattractive and functional walkway that led from the top end of the city down to the market area, providing a cheerful and ongoing vision of life within the timespan of the project. Artistic expressions such as these help to keep the dream alive as well as focused on the end result, through times of exhaustion and disillusionment.

In our secular society action can be an easier option than dreaming or praying because we simply do not believe that God is able to act in the world. We cannot cope with the intangibility of either dream or prayer. But action is no substitute, for without the dream and the sustaining power of prayer, our actions quickly feel empty. The rationale becomes 'since God cannot change things, then it is our sole job', while for others prayer just seems like a waste of time. But long-term dreaming the future into being requires the consistency of inner renewal, the faithfulness of perpetual prayerfulness, which remains vital to keep the vision alive. God invites us not to dilute our dreams by what we think is expected of Christian behaviour, or not to dream because it is considered wacky, or to become overwhelmed by a vision so unrealistic or massive that we cannot see it through. We cannot do everything, heal everything, transform everything. Our calling is to bring alive an area in our personal or corporate communities that feels dead, and simply to ask, 'What is God asking of me at this moment. Is this a dream of mine or is it the dream of others too?'

Art and other media have the capacity to generate hope and vision, often very simply. In the vastness and grandeur of Liverpool's Anglican cathedral, another building that proved a project over many years, Tracey Emin's phrase, 'I felt you and I knew you loved me' beams out in pink neon, providing an intimate vision in the immensity of that holy space. The cathedral, in which it seems impossible not to experience the love of God, is nevertheless a metaphor of the vastness of a world where people now often feel breathtakingly lost, where there are no longer any meaningful meta-narratives or spiritual backdrops to gauge and measure how to live life. In an article in the *Church Times*, Mark Oakley talks beautifully about the power of poetry. Poetry is primarily the language of the Bible, he says, which more appropriately uses words to describe the vision God has for the world, primarily described in parables and metaphors:

> The one whom we are to love most is the one whom we can never fully possess; so the language of faith is a language of increasing desire, ache and search. Poetry challenges religious literalism, encouraging our mind to think in metaphors, it asks of its readers a willingness to allow confusion to be part of the joy, and the seriousness of somehow letting language form you, more than inform you.[7]

146

Poetry would be an apt medium, then, to describe the idea of 'dream', for dreams are often uncrystallized, steeped in God's mystery but nevertheless generating the strong call to grasp the vision and see it through.

Living a prayerful life is to be people who dream in the widest sense of the word, people who believe in the authenticity of the biblical story, who have the courage to listen to the significance of our own personal dreams as well as being able to share and carry our own hopes and vision into situations that at first appear closed and airless. It is about being people who believe that the very process, even 'art', of dreaming is fundamental to our identity as followers of Jesus, and connects with an ancient tradition of somehow seeing a more positive future for our lives and for our church communities, and for the broken world at large. It is about being people who believe with a stubborn passion that through our prayers those incarcerated behind steel bars just might have a chance of release, and being people who allow God to live his dream within us so that it can be lived outside of us, turning life that is merely human into life that is more humane and exquisite. Living a prayerful life is about being ordinary people who have extraordinary dreams, with hopes to bring God's kingdom to fruition in a multitude of ways; it is also about developing the perseverance to see through the dream, like the story of the persistent widow in Luke 18 and the friend who came at midnight in Luke 11, both stories of how we need to hammer away at prayer and life until something blossoms or a breakthrough comes. Adrian Leak describes how the essayist Charles Lamb experienced the writer of *Pilgrim's Progress*, John Bunyan: 'If he came into the room, dreams would follow him, and that each person would nod under his golden cloud.'[8] There is no doubt that for generations of believers and non-believers alike Bunyan created a powerful allegory of our spiritual and moral walk through life with a dreamlike quality that punctuated many people's reality. In our own generation, if we as Christian people can aspire to such a description, to be those who 'carry dreams with them' wherever we go, in a way that brings hope and spiritual vitality to numerous occasions and contexts, we can indeed aspire to work with God to be a part of great things.

Dream in practice

Individual

- What are your unfulfilled dreams, big or small? Are these things you could see coming into being at a different stage in your life? How might you go about this? If they aren't, are you able to prayerfully put them to rest by giving them to God?
- Try keeping a record of your own dreams, as and when you remember them, or when you sense that a particular dream might be significant for you. Offer it to God when you pray and try to discern what God might be saying to you.
- Do you have a specific dream for your church or community? Can you talk to someone about this and can you identify other people who might share the dream with you?

Corporate

- Run a study group or sermon series on the dreamers of the Bible. The list might include Abraham (Genesis 15), Abimelech (Genesis 20), Jacob (Genesis 28), Joseph (Genesis 37—41), Samuel (1 Samuel 3), Solomon (1 Kings 3), Daniel (Daniel 2), Zachariah (Luke 1), Joseph (Matthew 1 and 2), Ananias (Acts 9), Cornelius (Acts 10), Peter (Acts 10), Paul (Acts 16, 18 and 2 Corinthians 12) and John (Revelation).
- In my experience, people relish the opportunity of vocational dreaming. Think of a simple and creative way for people to 'name' their dreams for their community, perhaps as part of a mission initiative. A graffiti wall is a simple and effective way of doing this. Ideas can be discussed corporately and

prayed through so that one or maybe two dreams can be put into practice. A colourful and visual method for a particular occasion, or to start a process moving, is creating lines of prayer flags, simply made by coloured pieces of material tied onto lengths of string. This is inspired by the original Buddhist practice which believes that these 'prayers' as symbols are taken by the wind when hung outside, and 'blown' around the world.

- Create a service around the 'dream catcher', an idea that originates in Native American cultures. It is a handmade object based on a willow hoop on which is woven a loose net or web. The original idea was to catch and trap any unhelpful dreams a person might have as they sleep. This concept can be translated to collect (visually or through art, poetry or photography) the positive dreams of your church or wider community.

Notes

Introduction: reclamation

1 Angela Tilby, 'Drawbacks of the super-dynamic', *Church Times*, 6 December 2013.

2 Christopher Jamison, *Finding Sanctuary*, London: Weidenfeld and Nicolson, 2006.

3 David Knowles, *The English Mystical Tradition*, London: Burns and Oates, 1961, p. 1.

4 Melvyn Matthews, *Both Alike to Thee: The Retrieval of the Mystical Way*, London: SPCK, 2000; *Awake to God: Explorations in the Mystical Way*, London: SPCK, 2006.

5 Matthews, *Both Alike to Thee*, p. 85.

1 Still: creating a still life

1 Caryll Houselander, *The Comforting of Christ*, in *The Hidden Tradition: Women's Spiritual Writings Rediscovered*, ed. Lavinia Byrne, London: SPCK, 1991, p. 118. Andrew Marr, interview with Robert McCrum at <http://gu.com/p/3hm5h>.

2 *The Observer*, 29 December 2013.

3 Francis Spufford, *Unapologetic*, London: Faber and Faber, 2012, p. 57.

4 Thomas Merton, Contemplative Prayer, in *The Fire and the Cloud: An Anthology of Catholic Spirituality*, ed. David A. Fleming, London: Geoffrey Chapman, 1978, p. 368.

5 From an article by Andrew Hunt in *Spirituality*, issue no. 86, Dublin: Dominican Publications, 2009.

6 In a story told by the Revd Rod Garner, *The Economist*, 1 February 2014.

7 Mother Maribel of Wantage, in *The Hidden Tradition*, p. 122.

8 Wendy Rudd, textile artist and teacher working in the Chester area.

9 Sister Wendy Beckett, *Sister Wendy's Book of Meditations*, London: Dorling Kindersley, 1998, p. 40.

10 *The Lion Christian Quotation Collection*, ed. Hannah Ward and Jennifer Wild, London: Lion, 1997, p. 232.

2 Gaze: the lost art of adoration

1 James Jones, quoted in Rod Garner, *How To Be Wise*, London: SPCK, 2013, p. 39.

2 St John of the Cross, *The Ascent to Mount Carmel*, Book 3, 22, quoted in *Lamps of Fire*, ed. Elizabeth Ruth ODC, London: Darton, Longman and Todd, 1985.

3 Thomas à Kempis, *The Imitation of Christ*, London: Medici Society Publications, 1930, p. 324.

4 Mother Maribel of Wantage, in *The Hidden Tradition: Women's Spiritual Writings Rediscovered*, ed. Lavinia Byrne, London: SPCK, 1991, p. 35.

5 Francis Spufford, *Unapologetic*, London: Faber and Faber, 2012, p. 208.

6 Jonathan Lawson and Gordon Mursell, *Hearing the Call: Stories of Young Vocation*, London: SPCK, 2014, p. 89.

7 *The Lion Christian Meditation Collection*, ed. Hannah Ward and Jennifer Wild, London: Lion, 1998, p. 111.

8 With thanks to Monica Thornton for this idea.

9 Martin Thornton, *English Spirituality*, London: SPCK, 1963, p. 208.

10 *The Lion Christian Meditation Collection*, p. 113.

11 *The Fire and the Cloud: An Anthology of Catholic Spirituality*, ed. David A. Fleming, London: Geoffrey Chapman, 1978, p. 345.

12 *The Fire and the Cloud*, p. 348.

13 Anthony de Mello, *Walking on Water: Reaching God in Our Time*, Dublin: Columba Press, 1998, p. 21.

14 Richard Rolle, *The Fire of Love*, London: Penguin Classics, 1972, Chapter 15.

3 Flux: holy hanging loose

1 Annie Dillard, *Teaching a Stone to Talk*, New York: Harper and Row, 1982, p. 150.

2 Rowan Williams, 'Renewing the Face of the Earth' in *Faith in the Public Square*, London: Bloomsbury, 2012, p. 186.

3 Richard Rohr, *The Naked Now*, New York: Crossroad, 2013, p. 23.

4 Thomas Merton, *The New Man*, Tunbridge Wells: Burns and Oates, 1996, p. 82.

5 Meg Wheatley, used in Chester Diocese *Headway* course on *Leadership through Discipleship*, session led by Canon David Herbert.

6 Banksy, *Wall and Piece*, London: Century, 2006.

7 Merton, *The New Man*, p. 126.

8 Timothy Radcliffe, *Why Go to Church? The Drama of the Eucharist*, London: Continuum, 2008, p. 207.

9 Malcolm Boyd, *Malcolm Boyd's Book of Days*, London: Heinemann/SCM Press, 1968, in *The Lion Christian Meditation Collection*, ed. Hannah Ward and Jennifer Wild, London: Lion, 1998, pp. 51–2.

10 John Dalrymple, *Costing Not Less Than Everything*, London: Darton, Longman and Todd, 1975, in *The Lion Christian Meditation Collection*, p. 270.

11 Dillard, *Teaching a Stone to Talk*, p. 150.

12 Quoted in Williams, 'Renewing the Face of the Earth'.

13 Prayer taken from *The Methodist Worship Book* © 1999, Trustees for Methodist Church Purposes.

4 Dark: containing and confronting the difficult

1 David Nicholls, author and screenwriter, quoted in an interview in *The Observer* Magazine, 29 December 2013; Richard Rohr, *The Naked Now: Learning to See as the Mystics See*, New York: Crossroad, 2013, p. 15.

2 Khaled Hosseini, *And the Mountains Echoed*, London: Bloomsbury, 2013, p. 322.

3 *The Cloud of Unknowing*, ed. James Walsh SJ, New York: Paulist Press, 1981, Chapter 3.

4 Helen Marshall, *Total Cost and Total Transformation: Learning from St John of the Cross*, Cambridge: Grove, 2011.

5 Olive Wyon, *On the Way*, 1958, in *The Lion Christian Meditation Collection*, ed. Hannah Ward and Jennifer Wild, London: Lion, 1998, p. 232.

6 Marshall, *Total Cost and Total Transformation*, p. 19.

7 Aron Ralston, *127 Hours: Between a Rock and a Hard Place*, New York: Simon and Schuster, 2010.

8 Constance Fitzgerald OCD, 'Impasse and Dark Night', in Joann Wolski Conn (ed.) *Women's Spirituality: Resources for Christian Development*, New York: Paulist Press, 1996, quoted in Marshall, *Total Cost and Total Transformation*, p. 17.

9 Carlo Carretto, *Letters from the Desert*, London: Darton, Longman and Todd, 1972, pp. 139–41.

10 Jim Thompson, *Stepney Calling: Thoughts for our Day*, London: Mowbray, 1991, in *The Lion Christian Meditation Collection*, p. 60.

11 Rowan Williams, 'Has Secularism Failed?' in *Faith in the Public Square*, London: Bloomsbury, 2012, p. 11.

12 Janet Morley, *A Heart's Time: A Poem a Day for Lent and Easter*, London: SPCK, 2011, pp. 42–4.

5 Stretch: stepping out of our comfort zone

1 John Pritchard, *The Life and Work of a Priest*, London: SPCK, 2007, p. 92; Brian McLaren, *We Make the Road by Walking*, London: Hodder and Stoughton, 2014, p. 254.

2 Rowan Williams, in Jonathan Lawson and Gordon Mursell, *Hearing the Call: Stories of Young Vocation*, London: SPCK, 2014, p. vii.

3 Timothy Radcliffe, *Why Go to Church? The Drama of the Eucharist*, London: Continuum, 2008, p. 198.

4 *John Sentamu's Faith Stories*, London: Darton, Longman and Todd, 2013, p. 19.

5 Rhidian Brook, 'Before Africa Reunited: Life, death and lessons in human kindness', *The Guardian*, 23 October 2010.

6 Brook, 'Before Africa Reunited'.

7 Graham Tomlin, *The Provocative Church*, London: SPCK, 2002, p. 30.

8 Tomlin, *The Provocative Church*, p. 114.

9 This image can be found in *The Christ We Share*, London: USPG/CMS.

10 Donald Osborne, *Pilgrimage*, Cambridge: Grove, 1996, p. 15.

11 McLaren, *We Make the Road by Walking*, p. 254.

6 Thank: an attitude of gratitude

1 Marcus Borg, quoted in John Lees, *Secrets of Resilient People*, London: Hodder and Stoughton, 2014, p. 167.
2 Rhidian Brook, *More Than Eyes Can See*, London: Marian Boyars Publishers, 2007, p. 181.
3 From a reflection by Professor Alyce McKenzie: 'A Thankless Job? Reflections on the ten lepers from Luke 17.11–19', at <www.patheos.com>.
4 *Letters from Ignatius of Loyola*, trans. and ed. William J. Young, Chicago: Loyola University Press, 1959, no. 55, cited in Peter Schineller, 'St Ignatius and Creation-centred Spirituality', *The Way*, 29(1), 9 January 1989.
5 Thoughts formulated from 'An Ignatian Path to Gratitude' by Wilkie Au, <www.theway.org.uk>.
6 Dietrich Bonhoeffer, quoted in *The Lion Christian Meditation Collection*, ed. Hannah Ward and Jennifer Wild, London: Lion, 1998, p. 192.
7 <www.gratitudegraffitiproject.com>.
8 See <www.gratefulness.org> for this and other articles by Brother David Steindl-Rast.
9 Steindl-Rast, <www.gratefulness.org>.
10 Thomas Merton, *No Man is an Island*, Tunbridge Wells, Burns and Oates, 1996, pp. 101–2.

7 Deep: where have all the wise people gone?

1 Rod Garner, *How To Be Wise*, London: SPCK, 2013, p. 20.
2 Garner, *How To Be Wise*, p. 4.
3 Sam Wells, *Learning to Dream Again: Rediscovering the Heart of God*, Norwich: Canterbury Press, 2013, p. xvii.
4 Philip Newell, *One Foot in Eden: A Celtic View of the Stages of Life*, London: SPCK, 1998, p. 77.
5 Christopher Cocksworth, *Wisdom: The Spirit's Gift*, Cambridge: Grove, 2003, p. 7.
6 Garner, *How To Be Wise*, p. 32.
7 Garner, *How To Be Wise*, pp. 47–8.
8 Garner, *How To Be Wise*, p. 49.
9 Cocksworth, *Wisdom*, p. 26.

10 Garner, *How To Be Wise*, p. x.
11 Brian McLaren, *We Make the Road by Walking*, London: Hodder and Stoughton, 2014, p. x.
12 Melvyn Matthews, *Awake to God: Explorations in the Mystical Way*, London: SPCK, 2006, p. 36.

8 Link: loving interconnection

1 Thomas Merton, from his final address during a conference on East–West dialogue in December 1968; Graham Ward, *Cities of God*, London: Routledge, 2000, p. 257.
2 Grace Jantzen, quoted in Melvyn Matthews, *Awake to God: Explorations in the Mystical Way*, London: SPCK, 2006, p. 54.
3 Matthews, *Awake to God*, p. 58.
4 *Church Times*, back page interview, 15 August 2014.
5 Thomas Merton, *No Man is an Island*, Tunbridge Wells: Burns and Oates, 1996, Chapter 1.
6 Merton, *No Man is an Island*, p. 1.
7 Sara Miles, *City of God: Faith in the Streets*, New York: Jericho Books, 2014. Quotations are from Sara Miles, 'Taking the ash outside', *Church Times*, 22 August 2014.
8 Melvyn Matthews, 'Thomas Traherne and the Reinvention of the World', Chapter 4 in *Awake to Thee: Explorations in the Mystical Way*, London: SPCK, 2006, p. 84.
9 Matthews, *Awake to Thee*, p. 127.

9 Shed: letting go and letting grow

1 Andrew Barton, *Decluttering: A Spirituality of Less*, Cambridge: Grove, 2006, p. 12.
2 Susan Hope, *Mission-Shaped Spirituality*, London: Church House Publishing, 2006.
3 Barton, *Decluttering*, p. 24.
4 John Miller, *A Simple Life: Roland Walls and the Community of the Transfiguration*, Norwich: St Andrew Press, 2014.
5 Angela Ashwin, *Faith in the Fool*, London: Darton, Longman and Todd, 2009, p. 100.
6 Anthony de Mello, *Sadhana: A Way to God*, New York: Image/Doubleday, 1978.

10 Dream: believing a future into being

1 Mary Grey, *The Outrageous Pursuit of Hope: Prophetic Dreams for the 21st Century*, London: Darton, Longman and Todd, 2000, p. 95; Walter Wink, *Engaging the Powers: Discernment and Resistance in a World of Domination*, Minneapolis: Fortress Press, 1992, p. 299.

2 Gerd Theissen, *Traces of Light*, London: SCM Press, 1994, p. 78.

3 Wink, *Engaging the Powers*, p. 298.

4 See Wink, *Engaging the Powers*, p. 299.

5 I am grateful to Lyn Weston for permission to share her story.

6 Brother Ramon SSF, *Forty Days and Forty Nights: A Guide for Spending Time Alone with God*, Grand Rapids, MI: Zondervan, 1993, p. 141.

7 Mark Oakley, *Church Times*, 3 October 2014.

8 Adrian Leak, 'Dreams would follow him', *Church Times*, 29 August 2014.

Bibliography

Banksy, *Wall and Piece*, London: Century, 2006.

Sister Wendy Beckett, *Sister Wendy's Book of Meditations*, London: Dorling Kindersley, 1998.

Rhidian Brook, *More Than Eyes Can See*, London: Marian Boyars Publishers, 2007.

Lavinia Byrne (ed.), *The Hidden Tradition: Women's Spiritual Writings Rediscovered*, London: SPCK, 1991.

Carlo Carretto, *Letters from the Desert*, London: Darton, Longman and Todd, 1972.

Christopher Cocksworth, *Wisdom: The Spirit's Gift*, Cambridge: Grove, 2003.

Annie Dillard, *Teaching a Stone to Talk*, New York: Harper and Row, 1982.

David Fleming (ed.), *The Fire and the Cloud: An Anthology of Catholic Spirituality*, London: Geoffrey Chapman, 1978.

Alison Fry, *Learning from the English Mystics*, Cambridge: Grove, 1999.

Rod Garner, *How To Be Wise: Growing in Discernment and Love*, London: SPCK, 2013.

Chris Gollon, *Incarnation: Mary and Women from the Bible*, London: IAP Fine Art, 2014.

Mary C. Grey, *The Outrageous Pursuit of Hope: Prophetic Dreams for the 21st Century*, London: Darton, Longman and Todd, 2000.

Khaled Hosseini, *And the Mountains Echoed*, London: Bloomsbury, 2013.

Christopher Jamison, *Finding Sanctuary: Monastic Steps for Everyday Life*, London: Weidenfeld and Nicolson, 2006.

Julian of Norwich, *Revelations of Divine Love*, London: Methuen, 1949.

David Knowles, *The English Mystical Tradition*, London: Burns and Oates, 1961.

Jonathan Lawson and Gordon Mursell, *Hearing the Call: Stories of Young Vocation*, London: SPCK, 2014.

John Lees, *Secrets of Resilient People: 50 Techniques You Need to be Strong*, London: Hodder and Stoughton, 2014.

Brian D. McLaren, *We Make the Road by Walking*, London: Hodder and Stoughton, 2014.

Helen Marshall, *Total Cost and Total Transformation: Learning from St John of the Cross*, Cambridge: Grove, 2011.

Melvyn Matthews, *Both Alike to Thee: The Retrieval of the Mystical Way*, London: SPCK, 2000.

Melvyn Matthews, *Awake to God: Explorations in the Mystical Way*, London: SPCK, 2006.

Anthony de Mello, *Sadhana: A Way to God*, New York: Image/Doubleday, 1978.

Anthony de Mello, *Walking on Water: Reaching God in Our Time*, Dublin: Columba Press, 1998.

Thomas Merton, *The Wisdom of the Desert*, New York: New Directions Publications, 1960.

Thomas Merton, *No Man is an Island*, Tunbridge Wells: Burns and Oates, 1996 (1955).

Thomas Merton, *The New Man*, Tunbridge Wells: Burns and Oates, 1996 (1976).

Sara Miles, *City of God: Faith in the Streets*, New York: Jericho Books, 2014.

Janet Morley, *The Heart's Time: A Poem a Day for Lent and Easter*, London: SPCK, 2011.

Philip Newell, *One Foot in Eden: A Celtic View of the Stages of Life*, London: SPCK, 1998.

David Osborne, *Pilgrimage*, Cambridge: Grove, 1996.

Grayson Perry, *The Vanity of Small Differences*, London: Hayward Publishing, Southbank Centre, 2013.

Stephen Platten and Christopher Lewis (eds), *Dreaming Spires: Cathedrals in a New Age*, London: SPCK, 2006.

John Pritchard, *The Life and Work of a Priest*, London: SPCK, 2007.

Timothy Radcliffe, *Sing a New Song: The Christian Vocation*, Dublin: Dominican Publications, 1999.

Bibliography

Timothy Radcliffe, *Why Go to Church? The Drama of the Eucharist*, London: Continuum, 2008.

Richard Rohr, *The Naked Now: Learning to See as the Mystics See*, New York: Crossroad, 2013.

Richard Rolle, *The Fire of Love*, London: Penguin Classics, 1972.

John Sentamu, *John Sentamu's Faith Stories: 20 Stories of Faith Changing Lives Today*, London: Darton, Longman and Todd, 2013.

Ray Simpson, *The Cowshed Revolution*, London: Kevin Mayhew, 2011.

Francis Spufford, *Unapologetic*, London: Faber and Faber, 2012.

Gerd Theissen, *Traces of Light*, London: SCM Press, 1994.

Thomas à Kempis, *The Imitation of Christ*, London: Medici Society Publications, 1930.

Martin Thornton, *English Spirituality*, London: SPCK, 1963.

Graham Tomlin, *The Provocative Church*, London: SPCK, 2002, 2008.

Hannah Ward and Jennifer Wild (eds), *The Lion Christian Meditation Collection*, Oxford: Lion, 1998.

Samuel Wells, *Learning to Dream Again: Rediscovering the Heart of God*, Norwich: Canterbury Press, 2013.

Rowan Williams, *Lost Icons: Reflections on Cultural Bereavement*, London: T & T Clark/Continuum, 2003.

Rowan Williams, *Faith in the Public Square*, London: Bloomsbury, 2012.

Walter Wink, *Engaging the Powers: Discernment and Resistance in a World of Domination*, Minneapolis: Fortress Press, 1992.